PBC
4.-
9/22

D1082899

YANKEE DRUMMER

YANKEE DRUMMER

By R. E. GOULD

Whittlesey House

McGraw-Hill Book Company, Inc.

NEW YORK : LONDON

YANKEE DRUMMER

COPYRIGHT, 1947, BY R. E. GOULD

All rights reserved. This book, or parts thereof, may
not be reproduced in any form without permission of
the author.

*The quality of the materials used in the manufacture
of this book is governed by continued postwar shortages.*

PUBLISHED BY WHITTLESEY HOUSE
A division of the McGraw-Hill Book Company, Inc.

PRINTED IN THE UNITED STATES OF AMERICA

CONTENTS

TOPSHAM FAIR

*W*HEN I was a boy and worked in a country store in New Hampshire, I used to envy the drummers, slick fellows who wore pressed suits with white handkerchiefs sticking out of their breast pockets and never seemed to do a lick of work. While my boss, old "Uncle John," as we used to call him, turned only one ear to these Knights of the Grip, impressing them with the idea that he was a tough customer to sell, I hung around as near to them as I could get, and while I measured off calico or scooped up sugar, listened to their stories of adventures on the road.

Probably I would have stayed right on in a store the rest of my life if I hadn't come down with rheumatic fever, chicken pox, and pleurisy all at the same time. The doctor slapped Spanish-fly plasters on my sides, and they raised such blisters that it was agony to move or even turn my head to be shaved. So I grew a Vandyke, listened to the doctor's warning that I wouldn't last six months in the store, and went back to Maine to buy a farm near the old one on which I grew up.

To make a little extra cash I did odd jobs, trading, selling farm machinery as well as real estate and whatever else came to hand, and soon managed to get myself into a tight spot with the machinery. The farmers in my neck of the woods had little ready money and paid for most of their purchases by barter. To sell a mower I usually had to take in trade a

1

horse or a cow or a few porkers and then turn them into money to pay my own bill with the machinery company. I did pretty well in sales, so well that I found myself with six heifers and no money. When the agent came around he was surprised to find no mowers or rakes but a barn full of heifers. I told him that if I had to pay the company then I'd have to sell all six heifers and lose my profit, but if I could keep them until the next spring I could settle the debt by selling only three.

"All right," he said, "the company lets you carry over unsold machinery until the next season on an interest-free note. I'll carry you over for six harrows."

From then on that drummer and I were fast friends, and I was so grateful to him that I was inclined to like the whole fraternity. A few years later, when he wanted to take over a Western territory, he high-pressured me into trying out his job. At the time I was doing pretty well with real estate, and I had cleaned up on so many farms for $500 and $100 down that I had practically sold myself out of business. It was getting harder and harder to find even a worthless pasture of bird's-egg gravel that would grow nothing but little gray moss-covered birches, and I hated to sell such land, even to a wise guy from the city who wanted to go into the goat business.

As a matter of fact, I never did like real estate. Nearly always your customer is a city-bred fellow who has a yearning to come back to the soil and doesn't even know which is the business end of a plow. He has a glowing vision of himself, in a wide-brimmed straw hat and bright new overalls, strolling about the plowed fields watching the corn grow, when you know that he won't be able to see the corn for the weeds. Then, too, he is usually an unsuccessful man who thinks that by changing the location he will better himself, but you know very well that his bad luck will go right along with him. So it didn't take a lot of persuading to sell me the idea of taking to the road.

Although I was afraid I couldn't fill the bill, I agreed to go to Worcester, Mass., for an interview with my friend's firm, the Richardson Manufacturing Company. A day or two later a telegram from the company asking me to come at their expense pleased me very much; but when I arrived and went in to see the president, Mr. E. P. Curtis, I was still doubtful about my ability to do the job.

Mr. Curtis was a wise old man who had worked his way up from office boy, and he soon made me feel more confident. He talked to me nearly all day. When he asked me if I had any recommendations and was told that I had none, as I had worked for only one man and he was dead, he laughed and said that wasn't a bad one. He gave me many tips about handling the trade and some of them I remember.

"Don't talk too much in making a sale," he warned me. "Lots of men talk themselves right out of a sale. As soon as you see that your man is interested, pull out your order book and get his name on the dotted line." Another was, "Don't try to tell the whole story. Leave something to your customer's imagination. Maybe he will imagine it better than you can tell it." He impressed on me the need of persistence, but I told him I was no hand to pump very hard on a dry well. Finally he concluded, "I can't tell you what to do in every case. When you get up against a hard one and don't know what to do, why, you'd better be at home." Then he told me I was hired and he would expect me to join the sales manager the next week at the Topsham Fair.

The salary Mr. Curtis offered me was pretty high for those days, so high that I pinched myself all the way home. After supper I was still so impressed with it that I decided to try it out on an old neighbor of mine; so I went over to visit him and found him in a rocking chair on the porch, comfortably smoking a pipe. When I told him I had a job for $900 a year and all expenses, he took his pipe out of his mouth and said, "That's more than I can make in ten years."

Topsham, a little town near the mouth of the Androscoggin River a few miles from Brunswick, is not a large place, but its fair is very old and draws from the surrounding farming country as large a group of lifelong customers as any in the state. Like all country fairs, it was the big sales mart where the farmers of the vicinity did their trading, and the companies who sold them supplies got their prospects for business during the coming year. The fair is held in October, when the farmer has his work pretty well in hand and feels that he can spare a day.

That week the leaves were in full color and the weather fine, as indeed it usually is, for Topsham Fair weather had become a proverb in Maine. I knew the country well and looked upon it as a piece of good luck that I was starting out at Topsham. Not more than five miles from there my great-grandfather and my grandfather, whose exploits had always prodded my ambition like a red-hot poker, ran a salt works during the Revolution. My great-grandfather was too old to get in the Army, and Granddad was only eight years old, so they made salt and sold it to the neighbors.

On a tidal arm of Casco Bay perched on a ledge at high-water level, my great-grandfather had built a row of stone arches to hold big potash kettles. Grandfather was an active, although maybe not too willing, partner whose job it was to feed the fires by sticking long saplings under the row of arches. At high tide he filled the kettles with sea water, which was boiled off to leave the salt.

The winter he was nine years old, Grandfather hitched a pair of young steers to a sled, loaded it with salt and a supply of pottery that was made by a neighbor, and set out alone into the northern farm- and woodland to do some bartering— a bushel of salt for a bushel of wheat or corn. When his supply was nearly gone he came upon a woodsman who had a pair of heavy oxen which he couldn't keep over the winter, as he didn't have enough hay to feed them. He wanted to trade them for Grandfather's young steers, which wouldn't eat so much. Grandfather had the sense to trade even or not at all, and furthermore he got the man to cut a longer tongue for the sled. He came home with a full load of supplies and a fine heavy pair of oxen worth nearly twice as much as the young steers with which he had started out. If he was such a smart trader at the age of nine, I figured I ought to be able to sell mowers and manure spreaders. After all, I had a lot of trading blood in my veins.

So as I drove into Topsham I was feeling fit enough to wrestle with a wildcat. Besides, I liked fairs; I always had since I crawled into the old Lewiston State Fair when I was twelve years old. The fat lady, the ape man, the scamps who run the concessions and have a hard time making suckers of the farm boys, the farmers surreptitiously looking over the madams and their girls and hanging around the exhibits of farm machinery never varied from year to year.

I never wanted to grow too old to enjoy fairs; but I realized that when we are middle-aged our impressions are not so sharp as they were when we were young; so, to keep my enjoyment fresh, I began that day a custom that I followed while I was on the road—I looked around for a couple of boys and took them in. It wouldn't be quite so much fun for them as my first fair was for me, because that time I got in free. The fifty cents for admission I had accumulated in various ways; but as I wandered around outside the fence, looking things over, I did a lot of thinking, for if I spent my money for a ticket I wouldn't have any left for other things.

Near me, on a platform for unloading cattle, a boy was standing on a board that leaned against the fence, from which he could look over. When he climbed down and crawled under the platform, I succeeded to the board and looked over too. Almost at once I saw the boy in the fairgrounds. Giving up my post, I crawled under the platform. Someone "without the fear of God in his heart," as Mother used to say, had dug a hole under the fence, a tunnel that led up into a manger filled with hay, at which a cow was chewing away as if she had never heard of boys crawling into a fair.

As I started through the hole I discovered another boy ahead of me.

"Be careful," he warned, "the man will tell you when to go."

In a minute came the word, "all right," and the boy went in. Then it was my turn. A man lay on a pile of hay as though he hadn't a care in the world. After a discreet wait he gave me the "go ahead" signal, and I crawled in.

If, when my earthly affairs are concluded and I hear Saint Peter say, "Come in," I feel half as pleased as I did then, I shall be surprised. And if he says I can't enter, I'll say to myself, "Well, I went to the Maine State Fair once and had an awfully good time, and it didn't cost me a cent for admission." I was loose in the fair with the whole of fifty cents to spend.

So at Topsham I gave each boy fifty cents and watched their fascination with a couple of Negro minstrels, a tall one with a banjo and a sawed-off one with an accordion. And how they could make those instruments talk! The big one played the banjo, and when he sang he opened his mouth so wide that he could have swallowed a whale. They were singing the same song that I had heard another pair of minstrels sing at that first fair:

> I'm goin' to the shockin',
> I'm goin' to the shockin',
> I'm goin' to the shockin' sure's you're born.
> I'll stay until the dawnin',
> I won't go home 'til mornin',
> I'll stay until the dawnin' shockin' corn.

One of the boys spent his fifty cents on a buggy whip. The salesman was doubling up a whip and stuffing it down his pants leg as he told how if you left your whip in the socket of your buggy while you were in church, someone would probably steal it, but if you had one of these whips you would be safe. Even if the minister asked you to lead in prayer, you could kneel right down and get up, and when you pulled out your whip it would be as good as ever. Then he would take out his whip to show that it wouldn't be hurt in the least by going to church in its owner's pants leg.

The other boy kept his money until he looked over the lifting machines, the shooting galleries, the fat woman, the snake charmer, and the striking machine that rang a bell when the striker won a cigar. He stopped to watch the man weaving silk handkerchiefs and one selling water wheels, and he stood for a long time before a case of sculpture done in butter. There were a thousand things to entertain a boy.

Finally I left my two guests at a bowling alley and looked up the Richardson tent, which was beyond the midway at the far end of the grounds, near the horse and cattle sheds. Several tents of other farm-machinery companies stood in line, but I noticed that our implements made the brightest display, for they were painted fireman's red, while the others were green or cream.

The sales manager turned out to be a bright, enthusiastic young man. He began immediately to coach me on our implements, the Buckeye mowing machines labeled $45, horse rakes priced at $20, and the handsome new Worcester Kemp manure spreaders at $120. We had a spreader on display and another jacked up on a couple of sawhorses and attached to a little gasoline engine to show how it worked. As I was instructed to sell this first and not bother about rakes and mowers until I got onto the work, I looked it over carefully.

While the sales manager was showing me how the spreader operated, he continued a running fire of instructions about the best way to get the farmer's signature or mark on a contract and sweetened them up with stories designed to kindle my ardor for the Richardson line. He was a great admirer of old E. P. Curtis, who had been the kind of salesman to make legends in the trade.

One of the old man's exploits, according to the sales manager, had to do with an important field trial of mowers in Bangor. All the leaders were represented: the Buckeye that old E. P. was selling, the Meadow King and the Clipper, the Sprague, the William Anson Wood, and many others that we don't hear of nowadays. On the great day when all were gathered at the field, there were no Curtis and no Buckeye. Just as the judges were starting the trial, a tallyho horn sounded and a tallyho with six white horses drove in and circled the field with a Buckeye mower towed behind and all the newspapermen in Bangor on top, also quite an assortment of beer and harder stuff inside. E. P. got off and unhitched the mower.

"Where is your team?" asked the judges.

"Haven't got one," answered E. P. "I'll get one of these farmers to hitch on."

"These horses are not used to a mower," cautioned the judges.

"I don't care," answered E. P., loud enough for everyone to hear. "I'd just as soon have a green team and a boy. Have you a team here?" he asked a boy who stood by, a barefoot fellow in a pair of old patched pants and a badly torn straw hat. The boy allowed that he had a team but they might not work on a mower.

"Don't worry," said E. P. "The mower will take care of that. All you have to do is to drive your horses and throw this thing over here when you want to mow, and back here when you want to stop."

By this time the crowd was interested to see a boy taking on a contest in which the others had the best teams that could be found. The boy hitched up his team, and everyone laughed; the horses were old skates and the harness was tied together with rope yarn and wire.

"Don't you mind them," said E. P. "You just tend to your driving and we'll see."

The boy trimmed the stuffings out of the others. With the blue ribbon flapping and the Stars and Stripes flying, the tallyho circled the field and drove back to Bangor. The reporters, with such a story to tell, plastered the front pages with a full description of the way the boy with the old horses and the Buckeye mower had swept the field. It was some time before the other contestants waked up to the fact that E. P. had brought the boy and the horses down from Massachusetts and planted them there. They had worked on a mower all their lives, and the boy knew more about a mower than the judges themselves.

"That's selling," concluded the sales manager in a tone that implied I could never hope to reach such heights but it might aid me to have such a mark to shoot at. Finally he impressed upon me the necessity of getting a signed order for each sale.

The weight-pulling contests were beginning in the field behind us, and the crowd was drifting past. We would get them after the interest in the contests slackened, so I watched, too, while their owners brought out pairs of oxen and loaded a drag with several blocks of granite. The first pair of oxen was hitched on, a crowbar was stuck in the ground back of the drag, and the timekeeper shouted, "Go." The driver shouted, and the oxen yanked the drag forward. The winners were the pair that dragged the granite farthest in two minutes.

Pretty soon the farmers began to wander back and hang around the implement tents, eying the new machinery the way the mare does her colt. One old fellow I knew; he felt well disposed toward me because I had sold for him a pasture lot that was so poor you couldn't keep a goat on it, but it had a fine view overlooking the river. He needed a spreader, and I knew he was good for it, so I got his signature on an order and also a note to pay for the following May. The sales manager couldn't see the need of a signed order if I had a note, and neither could I, but I wanted to follow instructions, so I took the order because he told me to and the note because I thought it best to clean up the job while I was at it. He agreed that I was right.

Looking back at it now I see that this was never the rosy life I imagined when I watched the drummers saunter in to clash wits with old Uncle John, but it had its good moments. Altogether it was hard work, with sometimes a little good luck to sweeten up my failures in the continual tussle with the sharp and cautious wits of New England farmers. No two days were alike and no two customers, so the variety compensated for knowing always that I was going to have scrambled eggs and toast for breakfast.

FISHING FOR A WHALE

At the fair I learned a lot about signing up a farmer. When a man hung around our booth and began to ask questions about our spreaders, it was up to me to find out what he needed and what he could pay. Our leading question was how many cows he kept; if he had quite a few, we sold him on the idea that he would save a lot of work and would increase the fertility of his fields provided he bought one of our machines. There was so much backbreaking labor on any farm that an implement which did away with some of the strong-arm work was always looked upon with favor.

If the man still held off, we tried to find out what was preventing him from buying. Usually the obstacle was money, so we had to put up a proposition that he could accept. Then he wanted to think it over and sometimes to talk with his wife. We counted on his being brought into the fold in a year or two.

Pretty soon I learned that our visitors fell into two classes: the farmers who did a lot of talking and asking questions and who liked to kid themselves with the idea of buying, although they had no more idea of spending the money than a grasshopper has of fasting; and those who stood around dumbly and looked at the shiny red spreaders and mowers with a goofy light in their eyes. They ventured a question every once in a while and then returned to their admiration. The first were bolstering up their own importance, but the second

11

would have that mower or spreader some way if they had to mortgage the milking stool to get it. They were the ones I starred on our list of future prospects.

The good bunch of leads that we got in this way was the foundation of the year's business. They were card-indexed, and a list was sent to the nearest local agent. Then a follow-up system kept tabs on them until they bought or died or moved away.

After the closing of the fair I received a list of prospects that had been turned in by an agent who had handled the firm's exhibits at the earlier fairs and was let loose in York, Cumberland, Oxford, Franklin, and part of Androscoggin Counties, a good territory, a farming belt that stretched from the Androscoggin River to the New Hampshire border. It was my job to call on our regular agents, usually the local hardware man or a responsible farmer who sold machinery to his neighbors, go out with them and help them make sales, and to find new agents in districts where there were none.

As I had been just such an on-and-off agent when I came back to the farm, I knew that most of these men were trying to make a little money on the side and couldn't be counted on to do much aggressive selling unless I could show them there was real money in it. If they happened to hear of somebody who wanted a spreader they might stir themselves to get his order; but they didn't spend much time going after new business, and when they had a tough customer they waited until the salesman came around to help them.

The implement business, at that time, was pretty hit-or-miss. A few old firms could be relied on to take a carload each of mowers and rakes, and we had many good old agents who took two to five mowers a year, but there were great areas that made me think of old Bill Smart's fishing experience.

In winter, Bill used to take the old mare down to the brook

to drink, breaking a way for her through the drifts and then getting behind to shove when she couldn't be persuaded to plow ahead. One day, when he was trying to get back his breath while waiting for her to drink, he thought he saw something under a log on the bank, so after he had hauled and pushed the old mare into the barn he went into the house and called to his wife, "Maria, where'n hell is my fishline?"

"I don't know nothin' about it," Maria called back from the kitchen. "The last I see of it was when the boys was goin' fishin' down on Moose Pond." After they had hunted for an hour or two, Maria found the fishline in the pocket of Bill's old pants.

Then Bill says, "Where's the fishhooks?" Maria didn't know. She 'lowed as how she hadn't seen them since he went fishing last spring and put them in a baking-powder can on the shelf behind the stove. But they weren't there. She and Bill turned everything upside down, and finally they came upon one up in the cupboard.

"What've you got for bait?" Bill asks. Maria said she hadn't a thing but an old pork rind. She sliced him off a piece, then he went out, cut himself an alder, tied on the line and hook, put on the bait, and crept down to the brook. There he could see the creature lying under the log. Bill kept back out of sight and threw that piece of pork rind in upstream and kinder let it drift down. The critter came out, grabbed the bait, and started back under the log. Bill gave a hell of a yank—but he *never got a goddamn thing.*

My first efforts in getting agents to handle our line produced much the same results as Bill's fishing. Sometimes we got a good agent, sometimes we got a poor one, and again we got one who was only fair. We were fishing for whales, but if whales wouldn't bite, we'd settle for a minnow.

I would get off the train at a small country town, look

over the stores, and try to induce one of the storekeepers to add our mowers and spreaders to his line. Usually I didn't succeed; country storekeepers were noted for their sales resistance. A lot of them were like old man Gowell of Lisbon Center. E. Swasey, one of my friends of the road, who sold stone- and woodenware, called on him one day and found him sitting in his store all alone, with his shelves practically bare.

"I guess you're glad to see me, as you are about out of everything," Swasey said to him hopefully. "You haven't any pails or brooms or washboards or bean pots or stone jars or clothesbaskets or clotheshorses," he went on, naming things that were the main stock of every country store.

Old man Gowell yawned and said, "Yes, my stock is getting pretty low, but business is kinder tough and I guess I can stand 'em off for a spell longer."

I found a lot of this kind, but they usually went broke after a while and made room for smarter, younger men. If I couldn't locate a good prospect in town I would go to the liveryman, and he would extend himself to think of a farmer who lived at some distance, so I would have to hire a team to go and see him.

Sometimes I found a man who really wanted to sell machinery, but more often I got one who needed a mower and rake and who embraced the chance to get them at wholesale. Occasionally I could stimulate him into making an effort to get some business; more often we got paid for our tools and heard no more from him.

At this time the chief crop raised on Maine farms was boys and girls, and it was as difficult to get money out of the farmers as it was to squeeze sap from a stone. Only in winter when they managed to sell some cordwood or logs or pulpwood did they have a little money to pay their bills.

My chief trouble on that first trip was my list of prospects that had been turned in by the man who showed the Richardson goods at earlier fairs. I didn't know it at the time, and I doubt that the company knew it, but this man had written down all the names he could get, regardless of their owners' needs or standing, and sent them in to make a showing. It was only luck that he didn't include children and the village half-wits.

I was turned loose with a list of prospects marked, "Will buy this fall sure," but as soon as I had gone around for a few days I saw that none of these prospects had either the means or the intention of buying, and it was a waste of time to go near them. Sometimes they had a farm and no team, at other times a team and no farm. Again they had neither one nor the other, or, if they had both, they didn't have enough ambition to run a spreader, much less want one. At first I thought it was my fault and worked harder and harder, getting up at daylight, hypering around the country behind old nags that were always dropping shoes or picking up stones on the way—and worked up a fine case of indigestion.

Although business was deader than a stillborn calf, I did get some pointers and no end of enjoyment out of our agent in West Paris. Roscoe Tuell wasn't very active any longer as an agent, and the company hadn't bothered to look for a new one even if he didn't do much business; but he had as many stories as a hive has bees. He was eighty-five years old and had sold our first Buckeye mowers nearly sixty-five years earlier, when no one in the neighborhood had seen such a contraption. The first one he loaded on a wagon and hauled about twenty miles to a farm where the men had just finished breakfast and were going out into the hayfields to begin mowing.

"I'm going to help you," said Roscoe as he unhitched his

horse from the wagon and hitched to the mower. The men stood around bug-eyed and leaned on their scythes as Roscoe drove the mower up and down the field and the hay fell in great swathes behind it. At length one of the men found his tongue and asked, "What would happen if you hit a stone pile?"

"I don't know," said Roscoe, "but I'll find out." He headed toward a stone pile about fifty feet long, which lay at the edge of the field, and drove right over it with the mower sizzling. When he drove back, the farmer asked cautiously, "What does it cost?" and was told a hundred dollars. That was a lot of money in those days; but the farmer thought he had seen a miracle.

"Come up to the house and get your money," he said, "and you can unhitch the mower and leave her right there in the field."

From that time until Tuell got too old to keep up his business, nobody else had a look-in on the mower business in that territory. As a matter of fact he had done too well for me, because nobody needed a mower or wanted to spend the money for a spreader. On one of my fruitless trips I came upon one mower that Tuell had sold forty-odd years ago. But the old fellow who owned it wouldn't listen to my proposition for turning it in on a new one, because it was working perfectly. I wanted to swap it because it would make such a good exhibit for the company, but when I wrote them about it they weren't enthusiastic. They had one so old that it had a wooden body and wooden wheels.

I had one prospect marked *urgent*. See him *this* fall sure. This was thinly populated country, a few farms, on narrow dirt roads that must have been almost impassable in the muddy season, and large patches of woods. After driving a couple of hours I began to wonder if I was on the right road, but there was no one to ask until I met a farmer who was coming out of a woods road with a wagonload of corn. He said yes, but I had still a long way to go. He was headed for the mill, which was along my way, and suggested that I stop there and ask the miller's wife to give me something to eat. He said that she often gave dinner to the farmers who came a long way.

Pretty soon we reached an old wooden mill and a dam over a shallow little river that came down from the hills. In a cleared patch cut out of the woods stood the house, a low building stretching out into barns and sheds all painted buttermilk red and weathered until they faded into the woods like dead oak leaves. We stopped at the mill, where the miller, a broad-shouldered, jolly fellow, helped unload the farmer's grain. Then I went up to the house to ask the woman if she could give me dinner.

She was in the kitchen rolling out piecrust, and when she came to the door, looked at me with a frightened air. At first I thought she must be the miller's daughter, for she was not more than seventeen or eighteen; but when she gave an anxious glance to a baby in a basket near the stove, I saw that she must be the mistress of the house. She was small and dainty and fluttery. Although she didn't hesitate to give me dinner if I liked beef stew and apple pie, there was an air of unsureness about her that made you feel somehow that she needed protection until she grew up strong enough to stand on her own feet.

She said dinner would be ready in about twenty minutes. She was just putting the pie in the oven, so I went back to the mill and looked after the horse. At the table the miller ate with gusto, scarcely noticing his wife, and exchanged jokes with the farmer, his great belly quivering with laughter. They were lusty jokes that most men wouldn't have told before a woman, but this girl didn't seem to hear. She fluttered about, filling the coffee cups, dishing out the stew, and cutting the delicious apple pie as though her mind was entirely on doing everything without a hitch.

After he had eaten a second piece of pie and downed a third or fourth cup of coffee, the miller pushed back his chair and said he must get to work. As he stumped to the kitchen door without a word for his wife, and we followed, I noticed a look of relief in the girl's eyes. She folded the dollar that I gave her into a little wad and thrust it in her apron pocket in an absent-minded way, as though it would mean nothing to her; but she thanked me gently and hoped I had enjoyed the dinner.

When we got back to the mill another wagon had drawn up and a big, overgrown boy was unloading.

"Now we will see some fun," said the farmer. "That boy's the biggest nitwit around these parts, and the miller always baits him."

As I was harnessing the horse I heard the miller's greeting.

"Well, Henry, you goin' to school this year?"

"No," declared Henry. "I know enough."

"You do, do you? Well, tell me what you know and what you don't know."

"I know plenty," Henry said, looking across the clearing to the porkers rooting in the miller's pen. "I know that you've got seven fat pigs."

"Fine," said the miller in a patronizing tone. "Now tell me what you don't know."

Henry thought a minute.

"Well, I don't know whose corn fattened them."

The miller turned as red as a turkey gobbler and made a lunge at the boy, but Henry was safe on the other side of the wagon. The farmer guffawed and winked at me as much as to say, "That was a bull's-eye."

The miller came to the buggy to see me off, and told me to keep right on the same road until I came to a crossroads post office. That was where the man got his mail, and the postmaster would know where he lived.

I said good-by and headed down the road that ran by the house, the pigpen, the barns, and into a little woods of cut-over pine and underbrush. When it took a sharp turn around a ledge of rock, I noticed a spot of bright calico in the path moving away from me. Drawing nearer I saw that it was the miller's wife, with a bundle in her arms. When she heard the buggy, she turned her head and fluttered into a clump of scrub oak like a frightened squirrel.

Stopping the horse, I called to her, for I could see her light dress through the bushes. Didn't she want a lift, I asked. She came out timidly, clutching her baby, and stood by the buggy for a minute, holding me with her enormous frightened eyes.

"No, no, thank you," she said. "I'm not going your way. Will you please not say you saw me, not to anyone at all, not even if my husband should ask you?"

I nodded. "But can't I take you somewhere?"

She shook her head.

"Remember, you promised." She ran back into the thicket and this time was out of sight.

There was nothing for me to do but drive on, and my common sense told me it was just as well I didn't help the woman run away, but I couldn't keep from thinking about the small frightened creature all the rest of the way to the crossroad.

On reaching it three hours later I stopped to check with the postmaster, who was sitting with his feet on the stove rail reading post cards. He said the man did get his mail there, but he lived a long stretch from the post office. With new directions I started out on his trail, but stopped a number of times to ask the way. At last, after I hadn't seen a house for two miles, the road ended. I was desperate; there was nothing to do but turn around and go back to the last house. At my knock a woman came to the door. She laughed when I asked her how to find my man.

"They should have told you he lives off the road," she said. "Go back about a mile and you'll see a pile of poles beside the road. Just beyond them is a gate. Turn in there and take the cart road, and after a while you'll come to another gate; open this and keep on, and you'll find him."

I did. It was getting dark, the fog hung low and dismal, and I was about all in, but the thought of a sure sale held me up. When the buildings came into sight they were welcome— although they weren't quite what I was expecting. However, I drove in, hoping for the best. A shaggy, bearded old fellow who looked more like a lumberman than a farmer came to the door and stared at me with surprise.

"If that don't beat all! What would I do with a spreader? I haven't got any stock or any team. I own 200 acres of pine-land and am just squatting here until the Saco people get ready to buy my pine."

It was late and the horse hadn't been fed. I asked the old fellow if he had any grain, and he said, no. He did have a little hay, which I gave the horse before we started back.

At about seven that evening I reached a hotel. They took care of my horse, but supper was over and I went to bed hungry and mad. Before I blew out the lamp I folded up my list of prospects and mailed it to the company, telling them that I was going to work one week more without prospects and if I couldn't do better than I had with these, I was going to quit. By that time I had grave doubts that I was cut out for a traveling man.

THE IRON RING

IT TOOK me a long time to go to sleep that night, and when I did, the tired horse kept clop-clopping through my dreams, going on and on down endless rutted country roads looking for a house that was always around another bend. But when I unglued my eyes the next morning and looked out the window, the day was bright and sunny. Feeling better, I took a train to Fryeburg, hired a team, and struck out along a road that wound through meadows of yellow grass and white birch groves along the Saco River.

Without knowing it, I had chosen my field of operations wisely. The Saco at Fryeburg makes a loop of forty-five miles and comes out almost at the same hole it went in. At the heel of the horseshoe was a good-sized pond that the early settlers proposed to connect with a loop of the river by a canal and thus reclaim the floor of the pond, which had once been the old river bed and should make good, fertile farmland. They asked permission of the legislature and were refused. Fortunately, the settlers had more sense than the legislators; they worked nights and dug a ditch to connect the nearest bend. When the waters of the pond were turned into it, they soon tore an outlet to the river, and the spring floods cut a channel that effectively drained the old river bed. Now the land that they reclaimed is as productive as any in Maine.

I started out early and by noon had fallen in love with this section, its pastures rolling over the low hills and its

21

patches of woodland flaming with red and yellow. It wasn't easy to turn into a farmhouse without even a worthless prospect card to tell you that the man was interested in a spreader, but I bolstered myself up by remembering what Father once said to me about the lion.

When I was eleven years old he sent me to town to sell a load of straw. It was the first time I had gone to town alone and the twelve miles seemed a long way, every yard strange and promising adventures. As I rode along on top of the load, I kept thinking about the circus that was in town and wondering if there was any way in the world I could dicker for a ticket. Each poster that I came upon further inflamed my imagination, until my hair was fairly standing on end when I looked at the tigers and the leopards on them, and especially the lions.

Suppose a lion should get loose! One of them might be loose this very minute, prowling through the woods. I had heard of such things. Sometimes they chewed up children before being caught and put back in their cages. I looked anxiously into the woods and wondered what I would do if the lion sprang out on old Prince and leaped on his back; would I try to fight him off with the pitchfork or would I run and climb a tree?

While I was trying to make up my mind about the proper thing to do, the road came out of the woods and skirted a deep, tangled swamp. This was even worse, for a dozen lions could hide in it. Suddenly a booming roar rose out of the swamp. It was the lion! Without wasting any more time thinking what to do, I whipped up old Prince and pushed him to his best lumbering gallop, scattering straw as we lurched along until we came out into open meadows.

I drove immediately to the square, where I saw Father's

friend the sheriff talking to some men. He looked at my straw and said he could take it all for the county if the price was right. I held out for five cents a hundred more than Father had told me, and the sheriff paid it without an argument. He even gave me a complimentary ticket to the circus.

Proud as a turkey gobbler, I strutted up to the ticket box with it, and before the performance opened under the big top, I listened to the barkers for the ossified man, the fat woman, and the snake charmer; I even wandered over to the menagerie, and there was the lion between bars, as tame as you please. That night when I told Father about my fright, he laughed at me.

"That same old bullfrog scared your grandfather fifty years ago. It just shows that it is foolish to be afraid of lions."

So I really didn't have anything to be afraid of now; there weren't any lions about.

I came upon a fine set of buildings and noticed on the barn the sign "Farm Implements for Sale." I turned into the yard and told my business to the man who came out of one of the cowsheds to meet me.

"Put up your horse and come in and get some dinner," he invited. The man told me his name was Chandler Buzzell. There was something direct and sincere about him. I liked his looks and felt he was the man we wanted. After dinner I went into more detail about our line and our discounts to our agents, and told him that with him as our agent I felt sure we could sell a carload of spreaders if we could put in a little time.

He agreed with me, but said he couldn't go along with me that afternoon, as he had to meet a man; if I would drive out and see what I could do, he would go with me the next day.

After dinner I drove about the country, stopping at every farm that looked promising. At one place the woman who came to the door said her husband was in the field, so I went down and showed him my catalogue. He needed a new spreader, and it didn't take much persuading to make him see that this was the time to get it; but we both reckoned without his wife, who came hypering across the field with her apron flapping and leaned over the fence to shout at us. She was a big, robust woman and her voice sounded like the trumpeting of a bull.

"I told you not to buy any more farm tools," she bellowed to her husband. "I told you I wouldn't stand for it." Then she turned on me. "You little no-account doorbell ringer, you have no business coming around here and selling him this stuff." I didn't know what to do. Remembering that Father used to tell me to keep away from an angry woman or a sow about to farrow, I just stood there and didn't say a word while she gave me the sharpest tongue-lashing you could imagine. She didn't climb the fence into the field, else I think I should have climbed the nearest tree.

"Now, now, Sadie," the husband called as he walked over to the fence. "Don't take on so. He was just showing me the pictures. We ain't done a thing."

But Sadie was suspicious.

"Every year you say that, and then you go get a mower or a spreader or a new cow, and I never do get my walnut parlor set. And I ain't a-goin' to stand for it any longer." She grabbed her husband around the neck with a clutch that nearly pulled him over the top rail, planted her head on his shoulder and burst into a fit of weeping that could be heard in Portland. He worked one arm loose and patted her shoulder.

"There, there, Sadie, don't take on so. I ain't done nothing.

This fellow was sent by Chandler Buzzell, who's going to be his partner. Don't you think we might give him a glass of cider?"

At the mention of Buzzell's name Sadie lifted her head and wiped her eyes on a corner of her apron.

"I've got some gingerbread in the oven," she said. "You come along in about ten minutes."

Sadie strode back across the fields with her apron, which had got twisted toward the back, flapping jauntily behind.

"Don't mind her," the farmer said when he rejoined me. "She likes to take on. You know, some people do, but it don't mean nothing. There ain't a better cook or a kinder-hearted woman in Maine than Sadie, and she thinks Chandler Buzzell's just about the best there is. Everybody does around here."

After the farmer showed me his stock, we went back to the house, where Sadie had set out a jug of cider on the kitchen table and a plate of hot gingerbread just out of the oven. She even asked to see a picture of the spreader and allowed that it might save her husband a lot of work.

After we had finished the cider the farmer took me into the parlor, where he kept his desk. We fixed up the contract, which he wanted to be made out for fall delivery and spring terms. I stuck it in my pocket and drove on, looking for other prospects, but had no more luck that day. When I returned to Mr. Buzzell's that evening, I asked him if the man I had sold was all right and if he would accept the sale. He said he would; the man was good for it.

"Did you meet Sadie?" he asked with a quizzical look in his eye.

When I said yes and commented on the esteem in which she held him, he laughed.

"There isn't a better woman in the neighborhood than Sadie, but she does like her tears."

After supper as we sat talking, he said, "I know a fellow who ought to buy a spreader." He went to the phone, called a number, and said, "Hello, Bill, here's a man who wants to talk to you," and handed the phone to me. I was somewhat taken aback to have the ball handed to me so suddenly but took a deep breath and told the man I was getting together a carload of spreaders for fall delivery on spring terms and we would like to have his order. He said he would take one as though he were just buying an ice-cream cone! I nearly fainted, it came so easily. Two sales in one day!

Next morning we drove out and saw a number of men but couldn't close a sale. Finally we came to four corners, and as we turned down a road I caught sight of a prosperous-looking group of buildings and said, "Why don't we see him?"

"You can't sell him," my agent said. "He uses oxen."

But I wanted to try, and he humored me, so we turned around and drove in. A young man who was at work at a woodpile said his father was in the house. I went in and told my story. The old man asked just two questions: "Can it be used by oxen?" and "When must I pay for it?" I told him that if he would sign the order, I would have the spreader fitted with a tongue for oxen without charge, and the bill would be due the first of May.

He said, "That's fine, we need it this fall, and I can sell a yoke of oxen in time to pay the bill in May."

I went out and climbed into the carriage without a word. As we drove off, Buzzell said, "I told you you couldn't sell him."

"I know it. Would you recognize his signature?"

He said he would. I showed him the signed order and he stared at me for a long time.

"I don't see how you did it."

I didn't either, but I thought it wouldn't do any good to tell him, so I kept still. We dug up another sale and then Buzzell said, "I want a spreader myself. That makes five. You can write an order for a carload, because I can sell the other two."

I wrote the contract, sent it, and the next day got a telegram from the president saying, "Good work." It was amazing to see how easily the spreaders sold, and I was feeling pretty satisfied with myself, not realizing, as I should have, the help I got from Mr. Buzzell. He was one of the finest men I ever met; everyone in his home town took his word on all matters, trusting his honesty and his shrewd Yankee judgment, and the very fact that he had taken on the agency was the strongest recommendation I could have had.

Some years later Mr. Buzzell was elected to the state legislature, where I followed his career. One day when I was in Augusta I went to the legislative chamber to see him. He was out, but I sat down in his chair and, while I waited for him, took a good look at our legislators, who were as unenterprising-looking a bunch of near idiots as you could pick in a day's drive.

When Buzzell returned we went over to the Augusta House for dinner.

"As I came in, you were looking around the chamber in a very interested way," he said, "and I wonder what you were thinking."

"I was thinking I couldn't see anyone that I would trust to water my cattle if I had to be away from home overnight."

He laughed until he nearly choked over his coffee. Finally he said, "I doubt very much if more than ten men have any idea of what is going on. They wait until someone votes, so they can tell how to vote, and the rest of the time they just sit and chew tobacco." Even so, the Maine delegation was a group of heavy thinkers in comparison with the New Hampshire legislature, which, he said, was composed of representatives from each village instead of from each district as it is in Maine. The New Hampshire lawmakers numbered about 500, and as the legislative hall held only 150, most of the solons spent their terms in the basement playing poker.

After the sale of that first carload of spreaders, I went on for a week or two, picking up a little business but no more carloads, so when a letter came from the company telling me to work a week as I had been doing and then report to the office on Saturday morning, it looked to me as though my days as a traveling man were over. I decided to make a swing north and west into the country around Sebago Lake and see if I could get some agents for the sale of mowers, rakes, and other tools that I hadn't tried to sell so far. At South Windham I hired a team, told the liveryman I would be gone a day or two, and struck out. I never repeated the feat of selling a carload, but I drove in new country, hunted up an agent every day, and made a good contract.

On Thursday it began to snow. I was in Dry Mills and had made a contract there, so I kept on. By midafternoon it was snowing hard, and by dark the snow was so deep that my horse had a hard time dragging the buggy through the drifts. Finally I stopped at a farmhouse and asked the farmer if he could put me up. He took me into the house and referred my request to an old lady who was washing dishes in the kitchen.

"Mother, can we give this man a bed and supper?" The old lady looked me over critically, then gave her son a crisp nod.

"Yes, I guess we can."

The bedroom upstairs was cozy and warm because the stovepipe from the kitchen passed up through it. The old spindle bed with its star quilt and the pine washstand with its flowered bowl and pitcher would make the antique dealers who scout our woods nowadays positively slaver at the mouth. The supper was more like a dinner, old-fashioned boiled pork and fried potatoes and apple pie. The old lady liked company and had set the table in the dining room instead of the kitchen.

After supper we drew up around the stove and talked. The old lady settled herself comfortably in an old swan rocker with a needlepoint back, put her feet on a footstool, opened her darning basket, and began to talk.

"What part of Maine do you come from?" she opened up.

When I told her that my mother's father lived in the neighboring village of Gray and that I remembered visiting him when I was a little boy, she rolled up her darning, pushed her spectacles back on her forehead, and took up a bag of knitting, which she could work on without looking. As her fingers began to ply the needles she asked me, "What was his name?"

"Why, of course," she said when I told her, "I knew him well, though I was just a little girl, perhaps your mother's age. His wife was a beautiful woman, and we girls always thought she was the most romantic person we ever saw. You know the story, don't you?"

I nodded, for Mother had told it to me in that same romantic vein. Grandfather had been an orphan, a village pauper; and as soon as he was old enough to work he had been bound out to the local rich man, who lived on the hill in what must in those days have seemed the height of luxury. There Grandfather learned the shoemaker's trade and fell in love with the great man's daughter. Nobody ever told me whether or not he had a hard time winning her, but he did marry her—although his father-in-law stipulated that his former bondsman must look after his wife with no help from the family. So Grandfather and his bride moved into the village, where he set up a shoemaker's shop. It was in this village house next door to the shop that I had visited when I was a boy.

The sharpest memory of that visit, a heavy iron ring bolted into the kitchen floor, had always remained a mystery to me. I could not see that it had any use, and I was too shy to ask. Now I questioned the old lady about it.

"Of course I know what it was used for. I have seen it many a time," she told me. "I shouldn't be surprised if it's still in the old house now."

When Grandfather was first getting established, she said, and times were difficult, he eked out his income by taking a pauper to board, a poor insane creature for whom the village selectmen paid $1.25 a week. The fellow feared only two men, Jesus Christ and Grandmother's brother, Joel Hinckley, so sometimes when he was unruly and insisted on tearing off his clothes, Grandfather had to send for Joel, a huge, black-browed man who subdued the poor fellow by looking at him. In the summer the pauper slept in the barn, but in the winter, Grandfather, fearing the man would freeze to death if he took a fancy to shed his clothes in the middle of the night, brought him into the kitchen and shackled him to the ring in the floor.

This old New England custom of renting out paupers worked in two ways. If the pauper was able to work, the selectmen charged for his services; if he was not, the village paid as little as possible for his keep. The old lady told me about a four-year-old orphan who was boarded by one of the selectmen for twenty-five cents a week. When the selectman presented the bill to the assembly, one of the other selectmen protested that the village shouldn't be required to pay it. Any four-year-old child, he said, should be compelled to earn his own living.

The old lady had a sharp wit and a vivid memory. I was almost sorry that the storm had ceased in the morning and the road was passable to South Windham. There I turned the horse over to the stableman, who refused to charge me for the last day, saying he appreciated my stopping over and bringing back the horse in good condition.

On the train to Portland, I kept reviewing these first few weeks and wondering how well I stacked up against the other salesmen. Not well enough, I was afraid. Probably the company was calling me in to fire me. They had given me my chance, and maybe I hadn't done well enough. The mail I picked up in Portland didn't tell me a thing, so I went on to Worcester in a depressed mood.

When I reported at the office, I laid the contracts on the sales manager's desk. He ran through them, looked surprised, and carried them in to the president. Neither one of them made a word of comment, either praise or criticism, to me. The sales manager called me into his office, gave me a little advice and a new list of agents and statements to collect, and I went out knowing nothing about my work except that I was a traveling man.

AROUND THE HORN

DURING the stay in Worcester, I spent some time in the storehouse of the company familiarizing myself with the stock. One of the first things I came upon was a big supply of old mowers piled three high in an ingenious arrangement and covered with dust that had not been disturbed for years. These were unsalable, I was told, now that the new ones had a ball-and-socket pitman head that did away with lost motion, the cause of much trouble in the old mowers. They were one of the company's mistakes; they had been made for foreign trade but did not comply with some of the requirements, and so had lain there for years.

Later I missed them and asked where they were. The sales manager told me they had been sold to a mail-order house and showed me the circular that the firm had printed to sell them. Although every word was true, I never would have recognized them from this glowing description; you would have thought the mail-order house had ransacked the world to find just what the prospective customer needed to make him happy. This advertising was a revelation to me, for this big concern was using the very same sales methods that we Maine Yankees have always used—only the other way around. We both stick to the truth—after all, why shouldn't we? I never could see why it is necessary to tell a lie when the truth can be just as misleading—only this Western firm went in for grandiose visions, while we stick to understatement.

For instance, when I was a local agent for mowing machines, I once took in trade an old machine, one of those inventor's dreams that never did work. All the blades cut separately, some idled while the others worked, and every ten feet or so one of the knives would break or come out. But I had to take it to make the sale. I figured I could get rid of it, so I cleaned it up and put it out before the front gate with a big sign on it, "Good as new, $5." Pretty soon the prospects began to drive in and ask about it.

"You say this is as good as new?" the first man inquired.

"Yes, it is," I told him honestly.

"Did it ever mow in the first place?"

"No," I had to tell him, "it never was any good—so it is no worse now than it was when it was new."

Naturally I didn't make the sale; but this man was the only one who asked me that question, so I got rid of the mower in less than a week.

I enjoyed spending this time in the warehouses, and it was necessary because the repairing end of the business was quite important, and I needed to know how all the implements worked. When an old-time Yankee paid $120 for a spreader, you can be sure that if it didn't work as it should, he would squawk until it was fixed. And usually he had to be fixed too, for he was always sure it wasn't his fault.

Somewhere on the road a letter from the company would catch up with me saying Farmer So-and-so was having trouble, so I would stop off and see what was the matter. Usually it would be something easy like a bolt dropped in the gears or the need of a few washers. When the farmer had run into an old bedspring and twisted his blades or dented them on a rusty old crowbar in the grass, I would have to send the mower in to the factory and pacify the farmer for his own carelessness.

My wife did not like these repair jobs, because she said they made me look like a tramp. When I came home from a hard week of doctoring machines that had gone wrong, she would meet me at the door with a mouthful of reproaches.

"Look at you! Look at your clothes! Why don't you have them pressed? Why don't you get shaved? Why don't you get your hair cut?" and much more of the same kind that I have forgotten.

"The last time I did that, a woman followed me around for a week and I had an awful time getting rid of her," I said.

"You know you lie; you never did any such thing," she would answer. Then we would both laugh.

But I sympathized with her. It wasn't too easy to be a drummer's wife, never knowing when your husband was going to be at home and never being able to count on him to take you to a church social, even a motion picture. It was almost as bad as having a sea captain for a husband, or none at all. But whatever came up, she never complained and always made the best of it. In the days when I was clerking for Uncle John and we didn't have an extra quarter, she had taken in boarders and stretched my bargain turkeys as far as a woman could. Now she took my phone messages, kept track of my routes, and calmed down the customers who wanted repairs on the instant and demanded to know when I would be at home.

When she railed at me for the way I looked, I would sweeten her up by giving her recipes for some of the good things I had eaten on the road. There was, for instance, the steamed clam broth that we used to get at the New Meadows Inn. I must speak of it in the past, for the inn burned down about twelve years ago. At that time it served the best dinner in Maine, which is one way of saying in the world. All you could eat for fifty cents! Every year a friend and I met at the inn for what we used to call the "Royal Gorge." Today I would wade for five miles through slush knee-deep to get another like it, and I wouldn't even ask the price.

The menu, which was as unalterable as the law of the Medes and Persians, began with lobster stew. After we had absorbed one helping, the waitress always asked, "Would you like some more?" to which my friend would wisecrack, "I sure would, but it might cramp my style when it comes to the real lobster." As for myself, I took the chance and always did consume two helpings. Next came the steamed clams with drawn butter and after them fried clams, not the kind you usually find at restaurants and that are as edible as last year's jar rubber, but the kind that have been fried by a friend of the human race.

When we got to the real dinner, on came big platters of plain lobster and lobster salad. After we had eaten about $7 worth of these, the waitress brought doughnuts and little vanilla wafers and ice cream and coffee. Oh, yes, I have forgotten the French fried potatoes with the fried clams. While I do not remember that I ever ate all I wanted, I always ate all I could possibly hold—and sometimes I overestimated my capacity.

Some years afterward, when the old inn was no more, I met the woman who had been the cook and learned how she made the lobster stew. Her secret was to use half milk and half clam juice, with double the usual quantity of butter to make up for the lost milk. "Don't use the big pieces of meat for your stew," she told me, "but dig out every little fragment with a nutpick. Also put in the tomalley, which is usually thrown away. Keep the claws and tail to serve as plain lobster, and serve the small chunks of meat as salad." Another tip she gave me was to be sure and salt the water in which you steam your clams, or they will lose all taste. Use the hot broth in your stew.

Not many years ago I followed this recipe when I put on a lobster supper for the Kiwanis. The next day I was called away from my work a dozen times by women whose husbands had insisted they find out how that stew was made.

But to return to the business of patching up old machinery, to which after all the lobster dinner was only incidental. On one of these missions I went to Sabattus, a pretty little village that lies at the outlet of a pond where the Sabattus River has its origin. These, as well as the neighboring mountain, were named for an old Indian chief who was ruling the country when the white man came. Rum soon became his favorite beverage. When a white man offered to give him all the rum he could carry in a bushel basket, he waited until a cold day in January and presented himself to the prankster with a basket that he had dipped in water and allowed to freeze until it would hold liquid. The legend doesn't say that the old chief got the rum, but I hope he did.

Old-timers claim that one time he was asked what he would choose if he could have three wishes.

"I would have that pond all rum and I would have that mountain all sugar," he replied without a moment's hesitation. After thinking a long while, he said for his third wish, "And then I would have some more rum." As Sabattus Pond is about five miles long, two miles wide, and 200 feet deep, he planned on a good supply if he wasn't bothered with too much company.

I found my old Sabattus farmer at work in his garden. He was sure the spreader was no good, and we would have to take it back. I looked at it and said that the return clutch had been set a little too far away and was slipping. It had worn the collar and needed a new one.

"You see," the farmer said, "it is impossible to put it on here."

I picked up two pieces of board and pulled out the cotter pin, tipped the spreader up, leaned one piece of board against the rocker, and, using the other as a pry, lifted the hind wheels off the floor. With the spreader resting on the end sills and my board, I took off the wheels and pulled out the axle, took off the collar, adjusted the throw, and put the thing together. It was all over in twenty minutes.

The old farmer was so pleased that he invited me in for a drink, and warmed by his rum, we soon began to talk about the general orneriness of the human race. He told me about the fishermen from Lewiston who came up in the summer and usually got drunk. They stole apples, robbed gardens, milked cows, tore down fences to build fires for cooking the fish, and went away, leaving the fires burning. All in all, they weren't popular with the farmers.

One day, when the farmer was at work in his garden, he heard a loud outcry from the pond and, investigating, found a boat overturned with two men clinging to the wreck and screaming for help. He rescued them, pulled their boat ashore, and turned out the water. They were very grateful; one of them grasped his hand and said, "You've saved our lives."

"Yes," replied the farmer, "but don't never tell nobody, will ye? The neighbors'll be madder'n hell with me if they ever find it out."

Leaving the pleasant old fellow, I went back to the village to scout for an agent and after a while realized that it was getting on toward dinnertime. I was directed to a boarding-house that sometimes fed transients. Dinner was over, but the landlady told me if I would put up with what she had, she would get me something. In a few minutes she set me down to one of the best meals I had ever eaten away from home.

For dessert she served an orange custard pudding that went right to the spot which had had an all-gone feeling for a long time. I asked her if she had any more. She did. She brought on a big dishful, and I ate until I was nearly foundered. When I asked her for the bill, she charged me twenty-five cents!

"Last week I had dinner at the Augusta House and they charged me a dollar. It wasn't half as good a dinner as yours," I told her, "and if you don't take this dollar, I am going to be mad at you."

That was the way in those days. You struck things very nice in some small country town, and in some of the big hotels you were likely to fare rather poorly.

After dinner I looked around to see if I could hire a team. The only one I could get was a pair of the meanest looking broncos you ever saw. But I was used to them; all the New England livery stables were stocking them and renting them to unprotected traveling men. For many years these tough little horses could be seen loping over the hills of Maine attached to a nondescript vehicle—they couldn't be trusted with one worth more than fifty cents. Their usual gait was about like that of a runaway horse.

Around 1900 some enterprising Westerner had hit upon the idea of capturing these wild ponies and bringing them East to sell at auction for what they would bring—and whatever the price, it was too much. One afternoon I went with a liveryman to an auction and watched the performance, which was almost as good as a rodeo. The sellers roped a pony with a coil of new half-inch rope and dragged him out for sale. After he was auctioned off at the highest bid, which might be anywhere from $2 to $25, the sellers cut off twenty-five feet of the new rope, fashioned a halter, and handed the end to the customer. Their trouble was over, but the customer's had just begun.

A couple of young Jews who wanted a horse to draw a junk cart bought a bronco for $3. When the cowboy handed an end of the halter to each one, the pony jumped back and started across the fair grounds, dragging the surprised men as if they were a couple of dolls. At the end of the field was a board fence some six feet high. The bronco jumped the fence easily and took his captors with him, but they hung onto their $3 worth and snubbed him so that they had him with his head looking over the fence at them and his feet on the ground on the other side of it.

I should have liked to follow them farther, but another pony was dragged up. Someone told me the story, but I can't vouch for its truth, that a man bought one of these horses, tried him out in a harrow team, and found that the bronco wouldn't pull, until someone suggested that he try the Indian method of tying the horse's tail to the harrow. The bronco worked that way very contentedly.

One particularly devilish pair of broncos was owned by a liveryman in Harmony and rented to carry drummers around the Horn, as we called the trip that started at Harmony and took in Cambridge, Wellington, Brighton, Athens, West Athens, and the Cornvilles. He didn't trust any of us to get them back safely and always sent along a boy who knew how to drive them.

One day when the roads were a sea of mud from a heavy rain, Frank Dennison of Bangor, who represented the Adams Dry Goods Company, started out on this trip. Frank was one of the most confirmed practical jokers on the road, a jolly fellow who always had to have something going on. Frank was getting bored; the boy who was driving was nearly asleep and the broncos were plowing along in the mud, not up to a thing. Looking around, Frank saw a barn coming into view with the front and back doors standing wide open and two men at work threshing beans. Pulling the reins out of the boy's hands and jerking the whip out of the socket, he lashed the astonished horses into a run, steered them into the open door, through the barn, over the beans spread on the floor, out the back door, and around into the road. As he went through he had a glimpse of two men trying to climb up the sides of the haymow, but, he added when he told the story, he didn't stop to see how they made out.

"I guess these nags are all right now," he said as he handed the reins to the boy. According to Frank, that boy moved over on the farther side of the seat and never took his eye off his passenger for the rest of the trip.

These same broncos jounced me around the Horn many a time. Although I never relieved the tedium of the trip by cutting any such capers as Frank's, I did have several adventures with these tough little beasts. One morning a young notions salesman, out for his first time on the road, and I were setting out from the inn at about the same time. The night before, I had tried to pull his leg by telling him a lot of whoppers about the best way to make a customer bite, but he was a bright youngster and not easily fooled. The next morning the liveryman said he didn't have a couple of drivers, so we would have to drive our own. As we looked over our rigs we couldn't decide which was the more rickety; his buggy had the paint kicked off and a great rent in the top, but mine had no top at all. His bronco rolled the whites of his eyes at us as though he would like nothing better than to show us his heels, and mine had so many ridges on his back that you could see somebody had had a disagreement with him.

We were both going in the same direction, but I got off first, as the boy had to make a call in town. I didn't expect to see him again, but as I was jogging along a dusty country road, well satisfied that my bronco hadn't kicked out the dashboard, I heard a yell behind me and, turning my head, saw that the boy was coming behind me, kicking up the dust in a yellow cloud. The road was narrow, so I drew over. As he came abreast he shouted, "I can't stop this damned horse."

My bronco, which had been plodding along with no special interest in life, gave his pal a jaundiced glance and leaped ahead like a shot. Down the road we raced in dust so thick that we could scarcely see each other. It got in our eyes and our mouths, and I felt that my whole alimentary canal was lined with it. I was hanging on stubbornly to the reins, but I had no more effect on that bronco than a sigh has on a cyclone.

I prayed that we wouldn't meet a team or be spiked on a fence post, and that the buggies would hold together. When we had been shooting along beside each other for what seemed ages but was probably five minutes, the other horse edged over toward mine, trying to cut him off, and the inner wheels locked with a splintering shriek. My buggy was tossed into the gutter, a wheel flew off, and I flew over the fence into the neighboring pasture. What happened after that I didn't know until a farmer ran out of a barn and picked me up. He dusted me off, saw that there were no bones broken, and then picked up my grip and took me to the house, where his wife gave me some warm water and patched up my bruises. He said he was driving into the village and I could come along; maybe we could find out what happened to the boy and collect the horse and what was left of the buggy. I was so shaken that I never once thought of trying to sell him a spreader.

As we came into the village we saw very plainly what had happened to the other buggy; it was piled up on the grass beside a little shop, and it looked like a handful of kindling wood. There was no sign of the horses, but I thought the people in the shop might know something about the young salesman, so I left the farmer and went in to ask.

A heart-warming sight greeted my eyes. The shop was a little general store; shelves of calico, everything from needles to footwarmers. In the middle of it, in an enormous rocker stuffed with pillows, sat the boy. His head was wrapped up until it was the size of a balloon, both hands were bandaged, and one foot was stuck up on a kitchen chair, resting on a pillow. Two old ladies were bustling around him, one with a cup of coffee and a piece of angel cake and the other with a paper and pencil.

"Two dozen pairs of cotton stockings, brown," the one with the paper was calling out as she made a note on the pad. "A box of assorted needles, one box of darning cotton, brown and black, one box of barrettes."

"Well, I'll be . . . !" I exclaimed. "What goes on?"

"Just getting an order," said the boy. His eyes twinkled, but his smile was lost under the bandages. "That consarned horse tossed me right into this shop, but this beats any way you told me of getting business."

MY LUCKY DAY

WHEN the company sent me to Somerville to see what I could do for our agent there, who needed help, I stopped off at the little town and found that our man was the local storekeeper. The building was not a prepossessing place; in front of it, emerging from the first drifts of winter, was an immense pile of old iron of all shapes and sizes, from old mowers to abandoned bathtubs, stoves, and junk of all kinds. Inside the store was about the same assortment and the same order, but the proprietor seemed to know where everything was. When a clerk said he couldn't find the twenty-two cartridges, the storekeeper went behind the counter, picked up an old stocking, ran his hand in, and came up with a fistful of the required size.

Around the stove a group of customers was having an impromptu town meeting about the fight the town was having with the railroad, the Wiscasset, Waterville and Moosehead, the only road that ran through that section.

"Has the town paid up yet?" I asked.

"No, and it ain't a-goin' to," the storekeeper answered, leaving a customer and coming over to join in. Then he launched into a description of the iniquity of the bondholders. It seemed that this railroad, a narrow-gauge road that the towns had helped to build with bond issues ("the Narrer Gauge," the natives called it), didn't work very well, charged high prices, and never did pay at that. When the towns were finally called upon to pay the bonds, Somerville lay down in the harness and refused to pay, saying in effect, "Let's see you make us."

The bondholders had the right to sell the smallest undivided part of the land that anyone would accept for the amount bid, although the original owner who had an equity remained in possession. In that state of affairs, said the storekeeper, most of the voters could apply for pauper aid at the next town meeting and those who remained would have to assume their support, while a certain group would vote themselves a good job at big pay and levy a crushing tax on the property and either collect it from the new owners or sell the property for taxes.

"Why, it got so the bondholders tried to attach our personal property," said one of the customers, "but we soon stopped that by a court decision. Then the bondholders began to attach anything that belongs to the town. The other day they attached an old road machine, even appointed a keeper to guard it. As soon as the sheriff was out of sight a bunch of the farmers around here who thought their road needed a shave and a haircut took it out, used it, and put it back in charge of the keeper, who was drawing good pay from the enemy for doing nothing very earnestly. It'll be a long time before they make us pay."

As I owned a piece of woodland near Somerville, I listened with interest, but when I saw that the discussion was going on indefinitely I drew the storekeeper aside and we got down to business. He said he had a customer who ought to buy a spreader, but he was so contrary that it would take a lot of work to get the sale. It didn't sound very good to me, but I didn't say so, and arranged to go out with the storekeeper the following day.

In the morning we set out behind a pair of frisky bays. It

was a gleaming spring day, and the storekeeper, who was a spindly little fellow, looked as ruddy as a pippin.

As we rolled along between pastures sparkling with early dew I kept thinking about Lion, Father's dog, who was the first pal I ever had. On mornings like this I used to go with him into the fields, hunting woodchucks. He was an enormous fellow, mostly English shepherd; and there was nothing in the world he liked better than hunting woodchucks. Every bright morning he ran out to the meadow behind the barn lot and lay flat near the top of a little ridge from which he could look over and watch for the woodchucks to come out of their holes and feed. Presently one would pop out and forage for a little distance, looking around warily, then dropping its head to eat. When it lowered its head, old Lion would creep up to the next rock or clump of bushes, then lie dead again when the animal raised its head to look around. His aim was to cut the woodchuck off from its hole. When he did, he would make a rush for the chuck, which would jump up onto the stone fence at the edge of the field and hide in the holes between the stones. When Lion had marked the spot, he would bark with such excitement and urgency that Father would leave whatever he was doing and go out to the wall to lift off a stone so Lion could get his prey.

But sometimes the woodchuck got to the hole first. Then Lion would plunge in and dig frantically. Often I have seen the chuck stick his head out at the other end of the hole and watch Lion's antics with ironical interest. When Lion looked up the creature would disappear into the hole with a taunting screech.

Every time Lion got his chuck Father put ten cents in an old baking-powder can that he kept on the mantel.

"Good boy, Lion," he used to say. "Keep it up. Pretty soon you'll have your license paid for."

It made me feel so good to think about him and how Father used to talk to him in the evening, pulling his ears and telling him big tales about the trades he had made during the day, that I concocted a whopper and sprang it on the storekeeper. I told him how Lion used to keep count of the dimes in the can by standing on his hind legs, lifting the can from the mantel, and tipping it on the floor. When there were enough dimes, he brought the can to Father and laid it on his knee. Then he didn't go after another woodchuck until Father drove him into the village and got his tag.

The storekeeper listened politely and never batted an eyelash. When I had finished he said, "Your dog sure was smart, but I don't think there's an animal living as smart as a bear. I remember one that used to get into the corn one fall when I was a boy. It ain't what a bear eats that makes the trouble, but it is what he destroys. He will stand up and gather into his arms all the corn he can grab, lay down on it and eat what is on top, then stand up and do it all over. A bear will ruin a lot of corn in a night, so my dad sent up to Lexington and got Uncle Bijah Luce to come and see if he couldn't ketch the bear. Old Bijah come down and brought some master great traps, but when he saw the tracks he said, 'I know this bear. I ketched him once up back of Lost Indian Pond, but he got away and lost part of his foot. He is mighty shy of traps. I'll try to git him, but it will take all I've got to do it.'

"So old Bijah went to work and he sot his traps where the bear came into the corn through a hole in the fence, and he covered the traps all up careful and then he took a spruce limb and swept over the traps to make it look natural. By that time it was dark and he was tired, but he wanted to be nigh so as to get up if the bear got in the trap, so he went to an old logging camp near by and laid down on the bunk. He was so tired that he went to sleep. When he waked up it was gettin' light, so he jumped out of the bunk and ran out of the door and landed square in those traps. The bear had come in the night and found the traps, so he took 'em up and sot 'em right where Bijah would step in 'em when he waked up."

I laughed as he had intended me to, but I couldn't help saying, "Who in hell is going to believe such a damned lie as that?"

"Well," answered the storekeeper, "you ought to. I believed your story, didn't I?" He had given me a lesson in politeness that I wasn't going to forget in a hurry.

We were both enjoying ourselves as the bays hypered along over the road, and we weren't too eager to reach our prospect, but after a while we came to a neat red farmhouse set back in a meadow, and he indicated that this was the place.

"There's your man," he said, "but I tell you he's the contrariest critter that ever drew breath." We found the farmer working in the barnyard, and as we came down the lane toward it I tried to size him up and didn't think he looked so tough. I had my speech all prepared and ripped into it with all the conviction I could muster as I pulled out the catalogue, but the man scarcely looked at the picture of the new Worcester Kemp and didn't spend a minute reading the description. He cut me short with a smile.

"I've been intending to get a spreader," he said, "and I have seen yours work. A hundred and twenty dollars, isn't it? Can I get it now on fall terms?" So as it turned out, all I had to do was to write the order, because he wanted the spreader and was in a hurry for it.

"Have you any more?" I asked after I had climbed in and slapped the lines over the bays.

"Yes, I know another, but you can't sell him yet."

"Let's go and see," I proposed, feeling pretty good.

We drove along the road a little farther and came to a

large farm with some fine buildings set back in a little grove.
A woman came to the door and asked us in. Her husband was
out in the cow barn, but she sent one of the children for him.
While we waited, she asked the storekeeper if the doctor had
got out yet. The storekeeper told her the doctor was in for
sixty days this time and wouldn't be out for three weeks.
The woman sighed.

"I wasn't feeling very well and wanted to see him, but I
guess I'll wait."

The doctor, she told me, was a fine man except when he
was drunk. Every once in a while, when he got out of hand,
the town fathers would send him down to Wiscasset to jail
for a spell, and it acted like a Keeley cure; though, as a matter of fact, the doctor was just as brilliant drunk as sober.

They both talked about the time he was summonsed to
court as a medical witness in a murder trial in Augusta. The
state had a big array of doctors on the stand, but the clever
defense lawyer so tangled them up that by night the doctor
from Somerville was the prosecuting attorney's sole hope, and
he was straining at the leash for a drink. The prosecuting attorney appointed a deputy sheriff to find out which one was
the doctor from Somerville and to ride herd on him all night,
never letting him out of sight.

The doctor saw the sheriff coming and guessed his errand,
so he pointed out a harmless old fellow. Then he went out
and got gloriously drunk, even in Augusta, the fountainhead
of prohibition. In the morning he went on the stand and was
a great success.

The woman said she was at the trial and heard him.

"We stick by anyone we like," she added. "Why, the
women around here won't even have their babies until the
doctor gets out."

Just then her husband came in from the barn and the

woman invited us to stay for dinner. The storekeeper's eyes brightened, so I took the hint and said we would be glad to. And I wasn't disappointed, for she served the best fried potatoes I have ever eaten. Although you may not have had the luck to taste them, I assure you that properly fried potatoes are something to rave about. What's more, they are fast becoming a lost art. Nearly all cooks dump boiled potatoes into a frying pan with a lot of grease and mangle them a little when they are hot. They call the result fried potatoes—but God forbid! Fried raw potatoes are a little better, but the only potatoes fit to be fried are baked potatoes.

This woman did them the correct way. She fried out fat salt pork, sliced her potatoes lengthwise about three-eighths of an inch thick, put them into the hot fat carefully, turned them when they were a golden brown, dusted them with salt and pepper, and when they were well browned took them out carefully to keep them from getting broken. The storekeeper attacked them as though he hadn't seen food for a week. I tried to be a little more reserved, but between the three of us men they disappeared like snow in May. The woman looked pleased, and brought in a custard pudding that made my eyes blink. I didn't see how the storekeeper could find room for it, but he managed.

After dinner we sat on the porch a while, and when I brought up the matter of a spreader, the man wasn't difficult at all. We happened to hit him at the right time; he had just bought several new cows and was wondering how he was going to handle the manure.

"Don't that beat all?" said the storekeeper as we went out through the front gate.

"Bring on another," I said, "but it may not be so easy to hook him. We've got to credit this sale to that wonderful meal." The storekeeper acknowledged that he did have another prospect but it was no use to see him. However, we did—and got his order. It was nearly traintime, so I gave a flick to the bays and said, "Have you any more I can't sell?"

"No," he answered, "I ain't goin' to take you to any more. If these fellows don't pay up prompt, I'm ruined now. Let's wait until they do, and then you come again."

As I drove back to town I began to feel that I was quite a salesman, although to be entirely honest I would have had to admit that all I did was to write the orders, as the sales were already made. A great deal of talk about crackerjack salesmen means that someone got a break. If you keep at it long enough you will get some breaks, but you will find also that doing and saying the right thing at the right time counts a lot.

A wise old traveling man once asked me, "What do you say when a man asks how you are doing? Don't forget that if he is selling the same trade that you are and is not competing with you, he is worth a lot to you. Tell him about a good deal that you have made or a new customer that you have found, and he will tell it to a dozen, and sometime when you go in to see a new man you will find your work more than half done, as he has heard a good report of you."

I always acted on that advice, as it sounded good to me.

OLD-FASHIONED WINTER

SNOW was no novelty to me, as I had been raised on a farm in the southern part of Maine, but I never had a taste of a real northern winter until the company wired me in February to meet the sales manager at the Snell House in Houlton. When I landed there, he told me that another man and I had been chosen to clean up Aroostook County. He gave me the part above Caribou, a strip that extends up the Saint John River to Edmundston and is the coldest country in the state, if not in the whole United States.

This is the part of the country that was inhabited almost entirely by the Arcadians, whom Longfellow wrote about so touchingly. But Evangeline and her friends were the dumb ones. The bright families had seen the writing on the wall, so they put their goods and livestock on a vessel, and sailed across the Bay of Fundy into the Saint John River territory. They pushed up to above Grand Falls and settled along the river for a hundred miles, where they live today as they did then. It is said that their cattle and horses are descended from stock brought over from Normandy 300 years ago.

This was the country of big woods and lakes, more lakes to the square mile than anywhere else in the world, but I couldn't see much of the woods or anything at all of the lakes for the snow, about six feet of it on the level and fifteen in the drifts. Signposts were covered, telegraph poles were about six feet above the snow, and houses were snowed in up to the second-story windows. Railroad trains ran in a canal that big rotary snowplows kept open by running nearly all the time.

After spending the night in Caribou, I inquired my way to Washburn, which was ten miles away, hired a sleigh, and started out. It was forty below zero, and my horse soon changed to white as the frost formed on every hair. There were no snowplows on the roads, which were kept open by driving on top of the snow and treading it down. Nearly all the traffic was by two-horse teams, although there were a few one-horse rigs like the one I was driving. These were of the setover kind, fitted with a device that allowed the shafts to be pushed over to one side so that the horse could travel in the track of one of the two horses that made the road, while the sleigh followed the sled track. It was a single-track road, but on every hill and sometimes oftener there were turnouts to allow teams to pass.

Soon I learned to wait at the turnout if a team was coming. These were potato teams dragging long sleds with bodies made of matched boards. The potato barrels, which were packed in tight, were covered with blankets, and under the blankets a small oilstove or several lighted lanterns prevented the potatoes from freezing. Believe me, they were a good investment that morning. If a man missed a turnout and met a team head on, I don't know what would have happened; but I imagine that if he ever turned out of the beaten road he would have been there until the following spring.

Finally I reached Washburn, put my horse in the shed, and went into the store, where a crowd of old-timers were discussing the weather around a red-hot stove.

One of them asked, "How cold was it up to your house?"

"Well, now," answered the other, "I can't just tell how cold it was. All I know is, my thermometer hung on the piazza and the mercury went right through the bottom of the bulb and right through the floor and, as near as I could tell, about six inches into the ground."

"Yes," commented a third, "this looks like an old-fashioned winter."

Another picked him up with, "What in tarnation is an old-fashioned winter?"

"Three days snow, three days blow, and three days colder'n hell," answered the first one. That is the best definition of an old-fashioned winter I have ever heard.

After collecting my account and making a small contract, I worked up through Limestone, New Sweden, and Stockholm, a section in which a group of Swedish settlers had hacked a swatch of fertile land out of the big timber. They had been brought over a generation earlier by our ambassador to Sweden, who happened to be a Maine man and was so impressed with the Swedes that he persuaded the State of Maine to offer them land. He set up a recruiting office in Stockholm and carefully selected the applicants, so the settlement in Aroostook represented the highest type of farmer and artisan. By the time I went to Aroostook a second generation had grown up. The old folk still spoke Swedish and the young ones had a strong accent, but their English was good enough to understand. They were very satisfactory people with whom to do business. I liked to stay in the spotless little hotels in their shiny villages.

Having cleaned up this district, I went on to Van Buren and arrived at about six o'clock, to find that the new hotel which had been built in the town hadn't been opened for business. The old one was a hotel in name only, but as it was a poor time to sleep outdoors, the proprietor was doing right well.

Ahead of me was a drummer from New York who was

selling ladies' wear. He emphatically explained to the proprietor that he wanted a warm room with a bath. The landlord looked at him as though he were an interesting bug and wrote down a number. I had learned not to ask for too much and said nothing. My room was fairly comfortable, but in the morning you should have heard that New Yorker. He must have spent a pretty cold night, for he told me his water pitcher was frozen solid.

The next day I crossed the river to Saint Leonard on the New Brunswick side, which is even more French than Aroostook, where one takes the train for Fort Kent. It was storming hard, and the train was three hours late. When it finally came, I quit the red-hot stove in the station and reluctantly found a seat in the chilly coach. We crept up the line with an engine that had a lot of leaky tubes and wouldn't make steam. About four miles the other side of Green River we ran into a cut that was full of snow, and the engine quit on us. It refused to go on or back, so there we were. A brakeman started back to Green River to summon help, and we resigned ourselves to passing a night in the wilderness.

Those of us who had fur coats, and that was most of the men, lent them to the women, several of whom had small children. We got through the night very well, although we were hungry, as we had had no supper and the same thing for breakfast. About nine o'clock I found three men who played whist and organized a game, which kept our minds off our situation for several hours. The other men seemed to be acquainted. My partner, a fine-looking man, and I cleaned up the others. As usual, someone started to tell Bible stories, and I told one about Pharaoh's daughter. It wasn't too bad. A minister who was examining a Sunday school class asked, "Who was the mother of Moses?" and a little girl answered, "Pharaoh's daughter."

"No," said the minister, "Pharaoh's daughter found Moses in the bulrushes."

"Yes, I know," answered the little girl. "That's what she told her father."

My partner laughed heartily and the others moderately. After the game ended one of the men took me aside and asked, "Didn't you know that your partner is a minister? He is the Rev. McCaskill of Fort Kent."

About noon one of the French Canadians aboard said he believed that if he could get out to a house, the settler would try to feed us, and if someone would lend him a fur coat, he'd try it. I lent him mine, and he started out. In half an hour he was back with the news that there was a house within a quarter of a mile, and if we would come over in lots of ten, the family would get us something to eat. We were to wait an hour to give them time to cook something. I never knew such a long hour in my life.

One of the whist players, a drummer who was selling crackers and fancy biscuits, tried to cheer us by telling us that in this French-Canadian country the people were the kindest in the world, especially if you stood in well with the priest, for they were very religious and the priest exercised a great influence over their every act. On one of his trips up the Saint John Valley, he told us, he struck Upper Frenchville on the day of the church picnic at Saint Agatha. As he couldn't do any business, he decided that he might as well go to the picnic, and so he did. As he was standing around watching the fun he was approached by an old priest who said, "I am glad to see you. Aren't you a stranger here?"

The salesman explained that he was just a drummer who had picked out the wrong day to come to town and thought he would attend the picnic and watch the fun.

"What do you sell?" asked the priest, and when the drummer told him, he asked to see the samples. The drummer quickly opened the samples and invited the priest to try the biscuits. The father turned to one of the storekeepers and said, "This one is very good. I should think you could sell some in your store."

"I'll take twenty-five boxes," said the storekeeper. Other merchants from near-by towns repeated the order until the salesman had made the biggest sale of his whole career. The storekeepers were taking no chances, as the fact that the priest had approved the biscuit made it a sure seller.

"Have you ever dealt with them?" the drummer asked me, and I acknowledged that this was to be my first experience, but we had some French-Canadian agents and I hoped to get others.

"Just because they haven't any education and mostly have to sign their names with a cross, don't make any mistake about their brains," he said. "For native shrewdness and a highly developed trading instinct, I'd back them against the Yankees any day."

He told me of a friend of his who stopped to look at a horse that a Frenchman had to sell. Her coat was a little unkempt but she seemed to be a good sound animal. The Frenchman assured him that she was.

"She's a damn' good horse," he insisted, "only she don't look very good." The drummer's friend bought the horse, but he hadn't got her home before he discovered that it was quite true that she didn't "look very good." She was stone blind.

At last the hour passed. We made up a party of men who had fur coats, and following the track made by the pioneer, we trampled down a road for the women. Finally we came to a typical one-story, two-room French-Canadian house, not more than fifteen by thirty feet by ground measurements.

The first thing I noticed was the stove, which was about five feet long and stood half in the living room, the other half in the sleeping room. The lower part was all firebox, and it took sticks of four-foot wood very handily. About an eighth of a cord was blazing away; a grateful sight to me who had helped tramp a road through a sea of loose snow.

The whole family was gathered in the living room: the father and mother, two daughters and two grandchildren, a little girl of two, and a baby. Three sons and the son-in-law, they told us in French (they didn't speak English), were in the woods up the Allegash River for the winter. The three women wore rough moccasins made by folding a piece of rawhide and stitching it into a rough outline of the foot.

The mother looked as if the cold agreed with her. If I had tried to hug her, I would have had to take a piece of chalk and hug as far as I could reach, make a mark, and then go around and hug some more. When I got home and told my wife about the family, I said that when the old lady wanted to reach anything on the top shelf she lay down, as she could reach higher that way than she could standing up. Perhaps I was exaggerating a little, but in spite of her size the old lady was a phenomenal cook.

She reminded me of Christ feeding the multitude with five barley loaves and two small fishes. She had boiled an immense piece of salt pork and about a bushel of potatoes and had made a bushel of doughnuts and a great supply of strong tea. On the floor stood a wooden pail filled with a mixture of some kind of meal and water, which I thought was for the hog, but the old lady seized the pail and gave it a few stirs with a big wooden spoon and then spit on the stove. Her homemade thermometer sizzled, danced across the stove, and disappeared. When the heat was right, she began to spoon out this mixture of buckwheat meal and water onto the top of the hot stove, and in a minute she had it covered with half an acre, or maybe a little less, of pancakes. She flopped a big cake onto a plate and motioned me to sit down. I did—and I can't remember a meal that ever tasted any better. We sweetened our tea with molasses and ate it on our pancakes.

When we had finished I asked what I should pay for my dinner, and learned that twenty-five cents was the price. The old man and his grandchild stood at the door as we went out. The little girl took the money and said "Merci" very prettily. Some of us gave her more, for we were grateful for the kindness of these people, who fed us of the best they had from their scanty store.

As we left I noticed the thermometer hanging on the doorframe. It registered forty below zero at midday, and I wondered how low it would be by midnight. I soon learned. In the middle of the afternoon a snowplow came up the line and pulled out our train. When we reached Clair in New Brunswick at about one o'clock in the morning we were turned out into the coldest night I had ever felt. The hotel was two miles from the station and there was no way to get there except by foot, but luckily my whist partner, who was met by a team, dropped me at the Dickey House in Fort Kent, across the river. The driver told us it was fifty-six below.

The Dickey House is a stopover place known to everyone who works this territory. Every drummer tries to make it for the week end, and when I arrived I found twenty ahead of me. To enliven the week end they had assessed each man $2 and had taken the proceeds over to Clair, where more liberal laws prevailed. They borrowed from a trader a thirty-gallon stone jar in which an old man they called Pop had made thirty gallons of punch that was stronger than any of the famous punches of Fitzsimmons. I was too late for the assessment, but that didn't make any difference; they invited me to the room where the festivities were being held, not once but a dozen times.

Several local men drifted in and joined the celebration. One little Frenchman who must have weighed about sixty-five pounds wanted to fight, and a big fellow who had driven a party up from Van Buren was willing to take him on but was restrained by the rest of us. At ten o'clock everybody was feeling happy; at two, several had retired from the field; and at five the landlady invaded the parlor, where one enthusiast was dancing on top of the piano. When she drove us out and locked the door, I went to bed, but all night some of the drummers were up trying to finish that jar of punch.

My next stop after cleaning up in Fort Kent was at Fort Kent Mills, to see an agent who had a stock of our mowers on hand. Some optimist had shipped them on consignment, and there they were. For years one of our men had gone up and, on discovering what a job it was going to be, had left it for the next man. This time I was the next man, so it was up to me to see what could be done about them.

The morning after the party, I started out with a one-horse sleigh and a local driver, and we hadn't gone far on the single-track road when we met a team of drunken natives who had driven past the turnout. It was still bitterly cold; I was muffled up in a fur coat, with the collar turned up, and a fur cap with the ear flaps turned down. The thought of getting out in that snow, treading a place for the horse, and pushing him off into it filled my soul with horror, but I was sure no words of ours could convince these men that they were in the wrong.

The driver shouted something. To my astonishment, the four piled out at once and in a minute had their horse out in the snow and their pung clear of the road. They took off

their hats and stood bareheaded as we drove by. I asked the
driver what in the world he had told them. He grinned.

"I just said, 'I got a priest wid me.' "

The agent, as I had been warned, was uncooperative; he
said he was too busy to help me and suggested that I let the
matter wait until warmer weather. When I tried to persuade
him to find someone else who could help, he said all the able-
bodied men were in the woods.

There was one man who could help me, and that one was
myself. I dug a canal through ten feet of snow to the door
of the shed where the mowers were stored, only to discover
that the door was of the sliding type and frozen solid. But I
thawed it out with hot water and at last got it open. Then
came my real trouble. The building was about a hundred feet
long, and the mowers were in the far end, with a million
shingles piled between them and the door. I wished I had
listened to my mother and studied for the ministry, but it was
too late then. In a pair of borrowed overalls I muled shingles
for two days until I had made a road to the mowers.

When I took a good look at them it was evident, as I had
suspected, that the agent had robbed these mowers to repair
others—a profitable business, for it used to be said that if a
man bought a mower at the price of repairs it would cost him
a thousand dollars. I went over the machines, listed the missing parts, found a teamster to haul them to the railway station, and shipped them to Worcester to be reconditioned.
Then I returned to the agent and presented the bill. He was
horrified. He said he would see the company and find out
what they would allow him, but I told him that I had instructions to settle with him and there was no discount—it was
cash on the barrelhead. After a long argument he weakened
and said he didn't have so much money. He finally offered
me $150 and a note for the balance, and as I couldn't see how

I could get any more money than he had, I took it and closed the account.

The next day I drove down to Upper Frenchville to look for an agent. Someone had told me that in their village the inhabitants cut their wood twelve feet long and stood it on end so they could find it in the winter, and I laughed at such a whopping tale, but it was a fact. In every dooryard a stack of wood stood on end, looking like a wigwam. Every yard had a hole in it leading down into a subterranean region. It took me some time to discover that the hole led to the pump, which had a house over it with a door opening in. When the house was buried, the villagers made these tunnels to get to the pump for their pails of water.

☆ ☆ ☆ ☆ ☆ ☆ 7 ☆ ☆ ☆ ☆ ☆ ☆

FRENCHMAN'S COUNTRY

IN THE section around Upper Frenchville we had no agent at all, so I went in to look for one. As usual, I went to the village store, hoping to find a suitable man in town; otherwise it would be a job for a beaver to tunnel a way into the country through the snow. The storekeeper didn't give me much encouragement about the village, which was just a few weathered log houses around an enormous church, but he did tell me about a smart and active young Frenchman who lived a few miles east of town. The man was a good farmer and had a lot of influence with his neighbors.

The road, the storekeeper said, was open, so I got a sleigh, rolled up my coat collar, pulled down my ear flaps, and started out. Not far along I came to a neat little house and barns dug out of the drifts. The Frenchman was in the barnyard, but when he saw me stop he came out to the gate and invited me into the combined living room and kitchen, snug and warm and neat as a pin. Shooing away a swarm of children, he made way for me to the stove, where I thawed and dripped like an icicle. Presently, when my lips had limbered up, I proposed that he take on our agency, saying that I had been told that his neighbors respected his judgment and I was sure he could do a good business. He was hard to convince, because the idea was new to him and he distrusted his own ability, but presently he decided to sign a contract for several rakes and mowers.

62

All this time the Canuck's red-cheeked young wife was busy about the stove. Every time she opened the oven door the aroma of a browning roast made my mouth water. Her husband invited me to stay to dinner, if I liked porcupine.

"You take good fat porcupine," he said, "you skin him, take out his insides, parboil him for about half an hour, den roast him, and, by God, you have chicken."

Although I had never tasted porcupine and didn't especially like the idea, I took a chance. And he was right. I asked him what else he could find in the woods or the river to feed his husky young family, and he said you could get sculpin and woodchucks, which were good enough if you cooked them right.

"Now you take a nice young sculpin just out of the water an' you skin him an' cut off his head an' tail, an' you take hout his inside an' you parboil him for half an hour wid little pinch soda, den you fry him in butter for ten minutes an' den you take an' make nice stuffin' wid bacon an' some more butter an' you put him in hoven an' bake him for about half an hour, an' den," he said with a fine shrug of his shoulders, "you throw him away. She's no damn' good."

"But woodchuck, she good," his wife said, "young woodchuck nice in the spring when she eat clover."

"Oui," he acknowledged with no particular enthusiasm. "You skin him an' fix him all up nice an' you parboil a while to take hout de strong taste, an' den you put him in hoven an' bake him for 'bout two hours. Me, I just as soon have chicken."

After we had cleaned up the porcupine I asked how the young man managed to raise such a large family and feed and clothe them on this little farm. His wife laughed and answered for him, "My fader have thirteen children and she say when hen have one chicken, hen do all scratchin' and when she have big lot, chickens scratch too." This, I thought, covered the ground very well. When I climbed back into the sleigh, warmed and encouraged by the hot dinner, I thought that with such a wife to help him the new agent would be likely to do a good business. And I was right; our relations with him were satisfactory over a long period of time.

As I learned more about these Frenchmen I saw the truth of the old saying, "Give a Canuck an old broom and ten acres of worthless birchland, and he'll raise a large family." He'll use the birches for firewood and from the wire around the old broom he'll make a snare to catch rabbits—and there he has his meat and fuel. For the rest, all the little chickens scratch. The women are just as resourceful as the men: they spin, weave, and knit (you might not want to wear some of their knitted underwear, but it is warm), and they can make a good dinner out of a root or two and a piece of jerked meat.

The greatest handicap of these people was their lack of education, which made them easy to exploit. Everywhere I heard stories about the way traders made money on the Frenchies. A man who sold wagons to them told me that he bought a carload in Amesbury, added ten dollars to cover freight and hauling, then doubled the price and hauled the wagons up the country, where he sold them to the Canucks. He took his pay in produce such as clover seed raised among the stumps on new-burnt land and threshed and winnowed by hand, allowing the farmer only fifteen cents a pound—although he sold it at Bangor for from twenty-five to forty cents. Also he picked up cattle in the fall and drove them to Portland, where he sold them for two or three times what he gave for them. The French farmers got small prices for what they produced and paid the highest prices for what they bought, but somehow they lived and grew up. There is one thing to be said for such a life: after a few years of it, nothing you find to do will seem hard.

I liked doing business with these people because they had a ready wit and got a lot of fun out of life. If they sometimes placed fun before the necessity of making a living, you can hardly blame them, but when you find one who tends to business, you have a jewel.

In Caribou we had a smart Canuck agent, a shrewd, capable man with a ready tongue; the whole countryside repeated his sayings. His answer to another farm-implement man who was trying to cut in on my territory was one of the favorite stories of traveling men all over the state. My competitor was trying a little soft soap by complimenting the agent on his family of fourteen handsome boys.

"You know, I would give anything to have one boy like these of yours," he said.

"Well," replied Mack, "I tell you what I do. You give me $50 and bring your wife up and let him stay one month and if he don't have a boy, you bring him back and it won't cost you a cent the next time." He usually had an answer for everyone, and somehow he managed to pack a laugh into it. There was never any malice in his wisecracks. In fact, I rarely met a Frenchman who had any malice in his nature.

In contrast with Mack was our agent in Madawaska, who was a shiftless no-account if ever there was one. He didn't even have enough gumption to deacon a barrel of apples, and that, if you don't know the language of the down-Easters, means putting the big apples on top to attract the customer.

But in matters directly touching his own comfort the man took no end of trouble. When his young wife died, leaving him with seven children, he went down to Houlton to prospect for another wife. There he met a young woman who listened when he told her what a nice home he had and what a smart man he was; he never mentioned the seven children. When the girl found them in her new home, she was game. She made them new clothes, sent them to school, and cleaned up the house and soon had it running in apple-pie order. When he saw that everything was going so well, the husband went and got roaring drunk, as had been his Saturday-night custom, came home, beat up the new wife as he used to beat the old one, and went to bed to sleep off his jag.

But this girl was of a different caliber. She waited until he was asleep; then she took a needle and sewed him into the bed, carefully stitching the bedclothes to the mattress. When he was well imprisoned she went out to the woodpile, got a club, and administered to him the father of all lickings. Her husband was so badly injured that she had to get a doctor to sew a three-inch cut in his scalp. As the doctor put in the stitches, the husband yelled at the top of his lungs.

"Shut up," the wife said. "The next time anyone sews you up it will be the undertaker, and that won't hurt."

The last I heard of the man, he had been a model husband for two years and hadn't touched even a glass of beer. Everyone thought the beating was just what he needed, but although it may have improved his manners around the house, I can't say that it made him a better agent.

Whenever we traveling men got together of a Sunday in a little village hotel in this section of the Maine woods and had nothing better to do, we would punctuate our games of pitch with stories about these Frenchies. On one such occasion a young man who represented the Oliver Plow Company showed me a letter that was sent him from his firm. The writer was a smart old Frenchman whose son was not quite so shrewd. When the boy arrived at the age of twenty-one, the father felt that he couldn't afford to lose the services of the son and didn't want to pay him a man's wages, so he hit on the plan of a partnership and had a sign painted on the barn, "Louis Michaud and Son."

The Oliver Plow man, who was out looking for an agent, found the son at home and sold him six sulky plows that retailed at about $50 each and got a contract signed by the son as "Louis Michaud and Son, by Henry Michaud." Evidently the son did not take his father into his confidence, for on the evil day that the plows arrived at the railroad station, the knowledge of his son's contract burst on the old man as a complete surprise. He sat down in his wrath and wrote this letter:

DEAR MR. HOLIVER PLOW:

I am surprise like hell when I go by the Rollrode and see what come by Louis Michaud an Son. He is dam fool and I ain't gone take him, so, Mr. Holiver Plow, you come to get him. She's come to most $300, and Mr. Holiver Plow she ain't worth 300 cents.

LOUIS MICHAUD.

I'm goin' tell you right now there ain't no more Louis Michaud an Son.

I countered with a tale of a Frenchman and a heifer that I had heard in Upper Frenchville. As a friend told it to me, a Frenchman in the village bought a heifer. After looking around for a farmer to winter her, he found one who agreed to do it for a dollar a week. By spring the bill had run up to a sum that was as much as the heifer was worth. The Frenchman finally suggested that the farmer buy the heifer. The farmer offered to take her for the board bill, but the Frenchman said that wasn't enough. After an hour or so of dickering he said, "I tell you what I do; you keep him two weeks more and you can have him."

Another told about a Canuck whom he met walking along a woods road carrying his gun with a disconsolate air.

"Hello, Louis," called his friend, "what's making you so blue? You shot anything?"

"Yes, my dog," Louis answered. "How I goin' to hunt rabbits without him?"

"Why in the world did you shoot your dog? Was he mad?"

"I guess he was," answered Louis. "He didn't act so goddamn' pleased."

All these tales came from Aroostook. When I was in the county again, it happened to be the November that Taft was running for a second term as President. On the day the returns came in I was in a little town below Caribou. That was 1912, the year everybody was talking reciprocity, and Taft had recommended that we admit Canadian potatoes duty free, an idea that was not too popular in Aroostook. As we sat about the store in the village hotel that evening waiting for the returns, I remarked that Taft was running better than I had expected.

"I guess you didn't expect very much," said a drummer with his feet next to mine on the fender. The next returns were those from the village itself, which gave Taft 1, Roosevelt 114, so the laugh was on me.

Near Fort Kent I visited an agent of ours, a merry, likable young Frenchman who had invited me to dinner with him the last time I was in the neighborhood. In his little two-room house I had met his inseparable friend, a big, blond Swedish lumberman named Johnson, to whom the thrifty couple had rented the bedroom. This time I found, to put it mildly, an atmosphere of strain in the little house. Again I was invited for dinner, but this time Johnson didn't show up, so I was curious to know what had become of him. After dinner the wife retired to the bedroom with a sulky look on her face and shut the door.

"What's the trouble?" I asked. "Aren't you and Johnson friends any more?"

"We just don't spik, dat's all," my agent answered. He shoved a piece of wood into the stove and poked it for a few minutes, staring at it with an expression of abject gloom.

"You know dat I go to work very hearly in de mornin' and dat Johnson he don't get up when I do. One day I get up an' eat my breakfast an' Hi go hout and she rain like hell and Hi go back to get my unbrella an' Hi try the door and she's lock an' Hi peek on the keyhole and Hi see Johnson kissin' my wife.

"Hi say, 'Well, she's good feller an' Hi hain't goin' make any troubles,' so Hi start to go to work again widout my unbrella, but, by gosh, she rain like hell. Hi never see it rain so hard, an' Hi say, 'By gosh, Hi got to get that unbrella,' an' Hi go back an' knock. When nobody open Hi pound on the door, for Hi got to get that unbrella. An' den dat goddamn' Johnson he come to the door and he open it an' he sees me an' he slam dat door in my face. Hi ain't speak to him after dat."

The Frenchman slumped in his chair and spat on the stove as he contemplated the unpardonable crime of Mr. Johnson, and there wasn't a thing I could say to comfort him. I never did know whether or not he forgave his friend for slamming the door.

On my next trip, as I took the train for Caribou I noticed across the aisle from me a Frenchman who seemed to be in trouble. Great tears were coursing down his cheeks and splashing on an infant that he held awkwardly in his arms. Every once in a while he reached over to the opposite seat and cuffed a little three-year-old girl, who let out a howl. Then the man would lean out the window, gaze back along the track, bring in his head, look around the car, and burst into fresh tears. When he had done this several times, I, who never know enough to mind my own business, said to him, "You seem to be in trouble. Is there anything I can do to help you?"

"My God, mister, I have more trouble dan you ever see," he answered. "Everything she go wrong. I have me nice farm down by Madawaska and I raise everything we need, potater, bean, buckwheat; an' I have horse, hog, cattle, sheep, an' all we want, an' I sell my farm like damn' fool an' go out by Kansas an' buy one of these goddamn' prairie farm. She's level an' she look nice an' I tell my wife, 'Rosie, by gosh, we goin' to make money here.'"

The man sniffed and rubbed his eyes with his knuckles. "I work like hell an' I plow him all up and put him into wheat and ba gosh she look nice. She come up all green an' she grow like hell, an' I say, 'Rosie, we goin' to make more money in one year dan we make in ten back in Maine.' De wheat she grow an' she begin to turn yeller, an' I say, 'Rosie, we goin' to make more money dan I ever see.' Den dere come dese goddamn' grasshopper bug an' dey eat up my wheat an' dey eat de paint all off my wagon an' off my house, an' pretty soon I ain't got nottin' but dese goddamn' grasshopper bug. But I say, 'Rosie, dis ain't no time to give up,' an' I get me a job wid my team an' I earn some money so we can eat. Den I work like hell an' I plow up the whole damn' business an' next spring I put him all into corn."

The baby whimpered and the man jounced her up and down.

"By gosh, dat corn she look nice an' she grow an' she turn green an' she wave in the wind an' de spindle come out an' de ear begin to set an' I say, 'Rosie, by gosh, dis time we got 'em licked.' About dat time come dese goddamn' cyclone an' blow my corn all down an' blow my barn into creek. I say, 'Rosie, we're licked,' an' I call hauction an' I sell every goddamn' thing I got an' take de money an' buy tickets back to Maine."

The man leaned over and gave the little girl another cuff that almost tipped her into the aisle.

"Now my wife Rosie she's gone and got a cinder in her eye, an' de goddamn' conductor he can't get it out, an' dis goddamn' kid has thrown de tickets out de window. Dese goddamn' brakeman she's got my daughter Marie, huggin' her back in dat seat, an' dis baby she's had a bad accident an' daubed me all up."

There wasn't a thing I could suggest to help the poor man— but soon things looked brighter; his wife returned and tended to the baby, the conductor was reasonable about the tickets, and the daughter appeared with a ring on her finger that was a lot too big but seemed to please her. When the family got off the train at Caribou they were met by relatives. The Frenchman looked up from the platform and grinned at me as though all his troubles were over.

GIDEON'S GEESE

*A*FTER that first Aroostook trip I was glad to return to my own territory, because that northern tip of Maine was not a cow country, and most of the farmers could handle the manure with a wheelbarrow. Then, too, the farmers in Aroostook were always holding potatoes for a high price that never came, and all you were likely to get out of business in that region was a flock of postal cards announcing that some of your debtors had gone into bankruptcy and inviting you to attend a meeting of the creditors. The attitude of the wholesaler was that of the Irishman who accidentally dropped a $20 gold piece into the collection box—"Oh, let it go to hell!"

But if I had counted on escaping from the cold I was mistaken, for winter was still in the Rangeley Lakes district over toward the New Hampshire line. The little towns were shut in by the big snows, and the wind howled down from Mount Blue like a dog with his tail in a crack.

On my first trip I planned to stay over Sunday at the Rangeley House, which I had heard was a good place for a man who likes his comforts, but when I got to Rangeley the big hotel was closed. Nothing was open but the Oquossoc House, which lacked practically everything of being a first-class hotel.

No sooner had I registered and shaken off the snow than

a drummer who was hugging the stove in the lobby told me his experience:

"Last night they gave me a northeast corner room, and I went to bed. I took off my coat and vest and my overshoes and shoes and got under the covers; then I got up and went into the next room and took all the blankets and comforts off that bed and put them on mine. After I had been in bed a little while, I got up again and put on my coat and vest, my shoes and overshoes, and my fur coat and cap. Then, after I had tried to warm up a while and was still shivering, I got up and took the rugs off the floor and put them on the bed. Finally I went to sleep—but tonight I'm going to sit up down here by the stove." However, I went to bed and toughed it out.

In Rangeley our agent was the owner of a hardware store. I had heard the story about the previous traveler for our firm, who had arrived there in the winter and tried to sell the agent a stock of spreaders. He wouldn't believe it when he was told that the country was not adapted to their use. Pointing out the window he said, "Look at these beautiful, level fields and tell me you can't use spreaders in this country!" The beautiful, level fields were the lake, frozen over and covered with snow.

At my next stop, North Anson, the hotel was old and the toilet was on the second floor at the end of a long hall. There was a stove in it, and everything was comfortable until you lifted the cover, when a blast from the North Pole struck you. This convenience led down into the barn cellar which was open on the north and reminded me of Chic Sale's North Dakota style of construction that was built for speed.

Not long after I had returned to the lobby to thaw out, a dry-goods drummer asked the location of the toilet and was directed. About ten minutes later he burst into the office with an expression of intense suffering on his face. He rushed to the stove and almost embraced it.

"Talk about the suffering during the war and the horrors Dr. Cook lived through at the North Pole," he groaned. "They aren't even worthy of being mentioned along with that toilet. My bones are just becoming thawed enough for me to really feel myself suffer. Why doesn't the management put up a sign warning everyone that he uses that toilet at his peril?"

It was tough, but not so tough as the one in East Baldwin. Here the innkeeper must have been a fiend for sanitation, for when I asked him where "it" was, he lit a lantern, handed it to me, solemnly led me around the house, and showed me a path that led out into the orchard. The outhouse was located about 200 yards from the house, and at one time I felt sure that a rescue expedition would discover my lifeless corpse, but I persevered. A line that I had heard somewhere kept popping into my head, "The chill winds of January howled around our lonely dwelling," but I'll bet they didn't howl a bit louder than the February winds that howled around the edifice in that orchard.

But perhaps my most bitter experience happened to me at the Mount Abram House in Kingfield. The clerk showed me to a room in which a little airtight stove was jumping and roaring at a great rate, doing its best to tear the hotel to pieces. It was filled with about six quarts of spool-mill waste that threw out a tremendous heat. I undressed in a warm room and said to myself, "In the morning I'll jump out of bed and start a fire; then I'll go back into bed and be nice and comfortable until the room is warm."

But the quick heat soon died down. In the middle of the night I wakened so cold that I was almost stiff. Climbing

out of bed, I ran to the big woodbox that stood by the stove
and opened it—to find not so much as a toothpick in it. By
that time my teeth were chattering so hard that I couldn't
curse the landlord for economizing on mill waste, which was
sold for ten cents a three-bushel bag.

Dressing as quickly as I could with numb fingers, I went
down to sit by the stove in the office. As I huddled over the
fire, a doctor who lived at the hotel came in from a midnight
call. He was bundled up in a fur coat and cap all covered
with white frost, each separate hair glistening with frozen
moisture. As he stood by the stove to warm up, another guest
who had been driven out by the cold came down the stairs.
He gazed at the doctor and asked, "What room did you
have?"

On another bitter night when I was toasting myself in
front of the roaring grate fire of a hotel not far away in
Stratton, I got to talking with my neighbor in the next chair,
a tall, rawboned, weather-beaten fellow of the Abraham Lin-
coln build. He told me he was a game warden who had been
called over from Washington County to trap a colony of
beaver that had built a dam across a stream near the village
and made a pond of it. They had flooded a lot of good tim-
berland. Unless they were trapped and the dam was broken
the trees would soon die, for a beaver pond kills everything
in it.

He told me that the previous winter he had been on the
Canadian border patrolling for deer poachers. Every winter
the French Canadians came over to the lumber camps. They
brought their own supplies but liked a little fresh meat, so
they shot a deer or two, although it was against the law. The
game warden went from camp to camp looking for deer meat.
The Frenchmen, he told me, had a saying, "You kill man, too
bad. You kill moose, five hundred dollars."

The Yankee loggers had a lot of fun with these Frenchmen trying to string them along, and it wasn't too difficult, because they knew so little English. One young Frenchman who had been told that Maine partridges were as big as turkeys went out hunting and came back with his eyes popping.

"You say partridge him big as turkey, my God, I shoot muskrat and him big as a calf." It was an expensive muskrat, for it turned out to be a beaver—and they are protected by the game laws.

Since the lumber camps were sometimes as far as forty miles apart, I asked the man how he had managed to carry enough supplies to live on. The warden said he carried very few, just a tea pail, a package of tea, some biscuits, a piece of meat, and a full-sized sharp ax. Living wasn't so difficult, but looking after yourself took a lot of time. At about two o'clock in the afternoon (it was dark by three-thirty) he began to look for a place to spend the night, the southern or eastern side of a hill where the snowdrifts are high. First he located a dead tree, which he cut, then several hardwood trees, which he chopped up for firewood.

The fire, after it got to burning, melted a hole in the snow four or five feet deep. When it was well started, the warden took off his snowshoes and made a cave in the windward side, lined it with the brush (fir made the softest bed), and cooked his supper. After he had smoked a pipe and was thoroughly warm, he took off his coat and covered himself with it. When he got cold during the night he waked up, built up the fire, got toasting warm, and went back to sleep. If a man went to sleep cold, he would never wake up.

Before he began to patrol the border, the warden was a trapper with a trap line up north on the headwaters of the Allegash. He trapped until mid-January, when the fur-bearing animals had all hibernated and there were none around except an occasional rabbit or porcupine and the hunter's pest, the wolverine. Then he dug spruce gum for the rest of the season, prying it off with a long, jointed pole tipped with a chisel. By March the snow became too soft for traveling when the sun was up, so he went to the forest at night and dug from the time it was light until ten or eleven o'clock, when the sun began to melt the snow. Then he holed up in a shelter that he had built at the edge of a smooth white plain, which he knew must be a lake or pond.

One afternoon, as he was half dozing in the shelter, he saw a beaver come up out of the middle of the snow plain. The creature was entertaining to watch, he cut cedar boughs along the edge of the woods and made a neat pile of brush by the hole in the ice, then he cut an alder, climbed up on the pile with it and sat there sunning himself, stripping the alder and having a good spring feed on the bark.

Suddenly a big white arctic owl, also looking for a nice spring morsel, swooped down from a hemlock and dug his claws into the beaver's shoulders. The startled beaver dived into the hole, taking the owl with him. A few minutes later the owl popped up and flopped to the top of the pile of spruce branches where the beaver had been sitting. He shook the water from his head, then stood on one foot while he shook the other. When he had smoothed his feathers he looked down into that hole, scolding and snapping his beak.

"He was the maddest bird I ever saw," said the warden. "Honestly, the way he snapped that beak I could almost hear him swear."

The warden told me the Rangeley Lakes are the finest trout-fishing water in the state, and I determined that the first time I made this trip in good weather I'd try to get in a week end of sport. Late that spring the company sent me back to Rangeley, so on Saturday after I had cleaned up my work I hired a guide and went out for a day on Mooselookmaguntic, the nearest of the six lakes. They say these were named after an Indian chief and his family, and I've often thought I'd like to hear the squaw call her brood to dinner. Mooselookmaguntic, Oquossoc, Molechunkemunk, Wolekenebacook, Cupsuptic, Umbagog. Try to say them quickly if you are looking for a tongue twister.

We fished up through the snags, a swamp of unrooted trees that had floated to the surface, and finally came out into a river where it was crossed by a railroad bridge plastered with a big sign, "Fishing prohibited under penalty of the law." The guide rowed right along, paying no attention to it whatever.

"Don't you think we'd better not go up here?" I asked cautiously.

"Oh, it's all right," he said.

"But I don't want to get into any trouble. Don't they have a guard to watch out for poachers?"

"You bet," he answered. "I'm the guard."

So under the guide's protection we fished along—and came back to the hotel with the finest mess of speckled trout you ever saw.

Having had such luck on Saturday, I planned to go out on Sunday to try the Four Ponds. To reach them we had to trek across a mountain by a trail that had been cut over recently. The lumbermen had left stumps sticking up and brush in the trail, and I never heard such proficient cussing as that from the guide while we climbed around in the undergrowth.

As we came out of the forest we saw a boy sitting on a stump, looking bewildered as though he didn't know what to do next. At first I thought he was an Indian, his face was so dark, but when we came close we saw that he was covered with black grease. He was wearing an enormous revolver in a fancy leather holster.

"That young fellow doesn't know as much as Gideon's geese," the guide commented to me as we came nearer and could see him more distinctly. "I'll bet that gun shoots a bullet as big as an early rose potato, and nobody ever shoots anything larger than a .32 in the woods."

"What about Gideon's geese?" I asked curiously. The guide looked at me as though I belonged in the first grade. Patiently he explained, "They were the geese that swam across a pond to get a drink of water."

When he saw us the boy looked up eagerly as though he was thankful for somebody to talk to. He told us that he came from Philadelphia, where his father was the editor of a newspaper. The doctor had told him he had tuberculosis and should live in the woods. The boy had invested in this firearm and come up to Rangeley. The first night he went to the hotel, but when he found out how much it cost he went a piece down the trail and camped. The next day, he went across the mountain to another hotel, but it was as expensive as the first. The manager offered to rent him a camp in the woods for $5 a month, so he parted with one bill from his slender roll and set out for it.

The guide let out a string of cuss words. That camp, he said, was an old, broken-down, abandoned lumber camp and didn't belong to anybody. Here the boy had lived for a couple of weeks on red squirrels and potatoes. If he was lucky enough to hit the squirrel in the head with one of his mighty bullets, there was sometimes enough of the animal left to fry. The black grease on his face, he explained, was a fly lotion with a tar base. Again the guide snorted and asked the boy if he had never heard of citronella.

All the time the guide was looking at that pistol with a

fascinated stare. He was like a baby coveting a piece of candy. I almost expected him to reach out his hand for it.

"Tell you what I'll do," he offered. "I'll board you four weeks for that gun." The boy's eyes lighted up; he was sick for a little human companionship.

We took him along, stuffed him with a big fish dinner, and listened to him talk. He had been bottled up so long that his tongue ran on like the chirp of a whippoorwill. When we started back he was pretty weak and could barely make the trail across the mountain. He unstrapped his cannon and let the guide carry it, and I saw that the big woodsman had already taken the youngster under his wing. I actually believe our finding him saved that boy's life.

But I didn't spend all my time around the Rangeley Lakes either listening to my teeth chattering or going fishing. It was the most beautiful section of Maine—which is to say of the world—but it was also fair farming country, too mountainous to compare with Aroostook County but still good. That spring I lined up a lot of spreader prospects, but I couldn't actually make the sales until August, for the company was so busy turning out mowers for the haying season that they couldn't make any more spreaders until they got rid of the mowers. So I said to all my prospects, "I'll be back in August and take care of you."

When I returned in August, all primed to do a good business, I was shocked to find that my first prospect had a brand-new International spreader, and so did the next and the next.

"Why didn't you wait for me?" I asked, trying to choke back my disappointment.

"Didn't you send this spreader?" they would ask, and I saw that they genuinely believed I had. "A man came through saying Mr. Gould sent him, so of course I thought he was your man and signed up with him."

It took me some time to smell out the rat in the woodpile. After a while I learned that the International man's name was Gould. How he found out about my prospects I never did discover, but I felt bitter about the whole thing. It would have taken more than a prophet to convince me that this man and I could ever be friends.

SCOUTING FOR AGENTS

SPRING was always a good time; there was a sort of expectancy in the air, and the farmers didn't seem so hard to interest in selling. But it was still hard to find agents, the right kind who would hustle. Sometimes I would have luck and discover a man in five minutes, and again I would drive all day without turning up a likely prospect.

At one village in which there never had been a good agent, I hired a team and went out into the country, stopping at each farm to ask the usual question, "Is there anybody around here who might be interested in selling farm machinery?" Before I had driven more than four or five miles, a girl who was clearing out a shed told me about a neighbor who sold sewing machines and might be worth talking to.

The place wasn't much farther down the road, an old farmhouse and several barns. No one was in the house, so I tried the barns. Opening the door of the first one, I found an old man standing and looking at ten colts loose in a big pen. They were rough and underfed but good; I could see that the old fellow had an eye for a horse. He told me he had picked them up for almost nothing and had wintered them cheaply. Soon he would get them out on good pasture, and when they had picked up he would cash in on them.

This, I thought, was my man. He invited me to come into the house and seemed pleased when I told him that the company would allow five per cent discount for cash.

"I can make a good thing out of it," he said. "I know all the farmers around here and what they are good for." He did, and he made one of the best agents we had.

In the next town we had once had a good man but he had died, and the new agent was squatting and selling repairs while our competitors were getting the new business. At the hotel in which I put up for the night I asked as usual for any ideas the proprietor might have, but this time drew a blank. He didn't know a soul who would make a good agent, but he did let me in on an entertaining story about his local boarders. Everybody was chuckling over a trick that had been played on the local banker, who was none too popular in the community. Neither was the local capitalist, whom we shall call Samuel B. Holbrook, who owned about half the place. Another Holbrook, who made his living by his wits and had a finger in a great many shady schemes, claimed to be a relation of the big man, a claim that was indignantly denied by Samuel B.

Not long before my arrival, the sharper had gone into the bank and asked for a loan of a thousand dollars. He had received the usual answer—that he could have the money if he would get a good endorser. He asked if Samuel B. Holbrook would do, and on the assurance that he would, the fellow took the note and brought it back in a few hours endorsed with the signature of Samuel B. The officers passed out the money, wondering if Samuel had gone insane or had been blackmailed into recognizing his kinsman.

When the note came due and the borrower gave no indication of paying, the bank notified the endorser. Samuel B. came storming into the bank and loudly denied ever having done such a foolish thing. The signature was a forgery. The bank officials then called in the maker to face the charge.

"Which Samuel B. do you mean?" he inquired blandly.

"I've got a boy named Samuel B." And so he had—a ten-year-old boy whose signature was on the note. The townspeople declared that the scamp had given his son that name for the express purpose of playing this joke on the bank.

In the morning I set out to find a new agent, and it looked like another long trip into the country. At the livery stable I asked the brisk young fellow who was hitching up a team for me where I could find a man who would like to sell my line.

"I want a man who will trade a mower for a cow or a flock of sheep or a wood lot; one who will be responsible."

He looked at me for a minute and asked, "How would I do?"

"Fine," I told him. "Then you needn't hitch up the horse."

He worked out well too, but sometimes I would drive for a whole day without turning up a soul who looked as though he could sell a piece of apple pie to a starving lumberjack. On one such day it was getting along toward dark and it was too late to go back to town, so I decided to ask at the next farmhouse if the farmer would give me supper and put me up for the night. It was a poorly settled road, with no houses in sight and no passers-by. Finally I caught up with a woman riding in my direction and asked her if she knew where I could spend the night. She said she lived about a mile beyond, and her husband would probably let me stay with them, so she led the way and we soon drove into a big farmyard. The woman climbed down and went to the porch, where she reached for the key that she had left over the front door. It wasn't there.

"It's that crow again," she exclaimed in annoyance. We heard a croaking on the roof and, looking up, saw a crow parading along the ridgepole with the key in his beak. The more the woman threatened and stormed, the louder the bird croaked in evident enjoyment of the situation. He would drop the key and watch it come sliding down the roof while he fluttered after it, cawing as though he were afraid he was going to lose it, but just as it was slipping over the eaves he would grab it and fly back to the ridgepole.

When this performance had gone on for about an hour the woman was frantic, and I was so hungry that I could eat a shingling nail. She kept saying, "Now you stand ready to grab it if it falls," but it never did.

At about this time her husband came in from the fields to do the chores and said he would be glad to put me up if he could ever get into the house for his milk pails.

"Just as soon as I get my hands on the gun I'll kill that damned bird," he thundered. "Look at him strut and brag. This time I'll kill him, and I don't care what my wife says. I won't have that damned thing around any more, and that's all there is to it."

At that, he threw a rock at the crow and came so near hitting it that the bird dropped the key in indignant surprise and flapped away into a tree. The woman opened the parlor and invited me in, but I went to the barn to put up the horse and gave the farmer a hand with the chores. When we came in, the woman said that supper would be ready in just a minute, but that before he washed up her husband would have to crawl under the front porch to get the spoons that the crow had hidden. I never heard a man swear louder, but he went and came out with not only the spoons but a gold watch that he had thought someone had stolen.

When he scrubbed up and sat down at the table, that crow was due for slaughter in the morning, but at that, the farmer wasn't feeling half so tired and depressed as I was after having driven all day without finding a single prospect. It was a delicious supper—ham, hot fried potatoes, corn bread, and homemade raspberry jam and a custard pie with meringue an inch high. By the time we had finished a second piece of pie, the farmer had promised to let the crow live a little longer, and I had signed up a new agent. If he put the same fervor into selling that he did into cursing, I knew we would have a good man.

That time it was a woman's desire to save the neck of her pet that made her cook a supper in a hundred and give me a break.

But once I was rescued by one of my stories that happened to go very well with the proprietor of a little general store in Franklin County. It was a bitter cold morning and there was a crowd around the fire in the pot-bellied stove. The proprietor was telling a story about the village bum, who had come in the day before and bought a quart of vinegar, a quart of linseed oil, and the same amount of turpentine, which he mixed in a gallon jug. When the storekeeper went home that night, he found that his wife had bought from the bum a pint bottle of furniture polish for which she had paid fifty cents. It was the same mixture that the bum had made in her husband's store. It works well, too; I made it and sold it afterward.

A lot of the customers were swapping stories, so I told a simple little one about Joe Gordon, an old employee of the Portsmouth Navy Yard. One time the yard shut down, and Joe had to go to Newburyport looking for work. Knowing that no private yard would employ a man who had worked in the Navy Yard, where the employees had a record for killing time, he said "No" when the foreman of the shipyard at which he applied asked him if he had ever worked in the Yard. He was hired, and as he was a good workman, he was doing well when one day another Portsmouth man came along. Seeing Joe, he inquired how one got a job.

"I just went in and asked," Joe replied.

The man went to the hiring office and when he was asked, "Did you ever work in the Navy Yard?" answered, "Yes."

"We never hire Navy Yard men," he was told.

He answered, "Like hell you don't. You have Joe Gordon working for you, and he never worked anywhere else."

The foreman called in Joe and accused him of lying, but Joe insisted that he had told the truth.

"I *was* there for a long time," he admitted, "but I never done a lick of work. You can ask anyone who was there."

Why the adventures of Joe should have seemed so funny to the proprietor I shall never understand, but he liked them so well that he went to the phone and began to call up his friends.

"Come over, Bill. Here's a fellow that's got a story for you."

Until noon I sat there repeating the story. When the proprietor couldn't think of another friend who hadn't heard it, he asked me, "What in hell do you sell, anyhow?"

"The Buckeye mower," I told him. He gave me an order for half a dozen.

On the other hand I remember one trip that should have been a good one but was a complete failure. Our agent over in Franklin County, a smart old veterinary surgeon who knew everyone in the countryside, was very successful. It was mudtime when we started out on a trip together to clean up some prospects. We were driving his stallion, a remarkably fine horse, so good that I wondered how it happened to be in his possession. He told me that he had bought the horse as a colt for $10 when it was injured in a train wreck. The vet amputated the end of the stallion's lower jaw and saved him, but they had to feed him a bran mash as the horse couldn't bite anything.

All day we traveled without nailing a single order, and we were both pretty glum when we got an indifferent supper at a farmhouse and started back over the mountains in the dark. As we turned into the road, the old man handed me the reins and asked me to drive because he couldn't see the road. I didn't tell him so, but I couldn't see it either. The horse didn't like to walk in the mud, and when the going got tough he would move over and walk on the grass border. This would throw our wheels out of the tracks, so after a while when I failed to hear his feet sucking as he pulled them out of the mud, I would know that he was walking on the grass and pull him back. We had driven this way several miles when I saw a light in a farmhouse and stopped to borrow a lantern. A few feet ahead I could see the driveway, which was a lighter color than the rest. Just as I stepped off the road I felt that something was wrong, so I lit my last match to have a look. I was standing on a culvert and my "driveway" was a brook.

A few feet farther on I discovered the real driveway and suggested to the vet that I walk up; it would take only a few minutes. He nodded and took the reins, and as I plunged off into the dark I could smell that he had bitten off a comforting chew of tobacco. Squdging along in the mud that I could feel but not see, I reached the house and saw that the light was coming from the kitchen, where a couple of men sat over a jug of cider. The one who answered my knock said he would be glad to let me have a lantern if I'd wait a minute until he convinced his friend that a sow was smarter than a horse. He poured me a mug of cider—and in spite of my misgivings about keeping the vet waiting, I did enjoy it. But the argument, I soon saw, was one-sided and likely to last indefinitely, as the friend was too sleepy to interrupt the farmer's monologue.

The farmer was telling about an old sow of his that was

very clever about getting out of the pen into the pasture. In the pen fence she had discovered two boards that were nailed together with a single nail. By running her snout between the boards, she could pry them apart enough to squeeze through. Then they would spring together and she couldn't get back into the pen—but she didn't care, because she was free until somebody rounded her up and drove her in. The farmer maintained that she was the smartest animal on the place, because she never tried to get out when anybody was looking. It took him weeks to find out how she did it, and he might never have known if he hadn't heard the smack of the boards as they fell back together.

I told him about a sow that I had spent many a day chasing when I was a boy on my father's farm. Our fence around the hog lot was of logs. The sow had discovered a hollow one that had a bend in it, so that the other end stuck out into the field. By wriggling and pushing she could just get through. After I hid behind the fence a few days and discovered how she did it I turned the log around so that both ends opened in the hog lot; then I watched her squeeze through. When she came out in the pen instead of the field she looked around in surprise and tried again. After she had made the trip the third time and still came out in the pen, she put up her tail, snorted, woosch-woosch, and trotted off. I always thought she was just as smart to refuse to worry about her failure as she was to find the log in the first place.

By this time the champion of the horse had slumped down with his head on the table. I suggested that I'd be glad to have the lantern, since a friend was waiting in the buggy. The farmer took one down from a nail by the kitchen door, looked to see that it was filled with oil, and left the door open to light me down the drive. The old vet was fast asleep. He was cross when I wakened him and grumbled all the way home, but after we had reached his house at about midnight and put up the stallion, he poured us a drink of Newburyport rum and cheered up remarkably.

"It's a good thing I had you with me," he said. "I haven't seen a thing for the last ten miles." I didn't say so, but I hadn't seen anything either.

By the time I reached South Paris the sun had been out for a couple of days and the mud had dried. When I drove out early in the morning to pick up my agent for a day of canvassing, the air was soft with spring and Maine was a lovely place.

At about eight o'clock I pulled up at the man's house and found him gone, but his family was in the road looking toward a patch of woods and whispering in great agitation. His wife told me that the man who lived next door had quarreled with his family the previous evening and had rushed out into the woods. He didn't come back all night. In the morning his family went out to look for him and found him hanging from a tree. They had run next door to my agent for help, and he had gone with them to bring the body home. People were gathering in front of the house, standing about and whispering together. Just then a crowd came out of the woods with the body and carried it into the house. We could hear their weeping; all the people in front of the house began to lament, and the sound of their wailing could be heard a mile away.

A little while later the agent came home to see if I had arrived.

"You won't want to go out canvassing after this trying experience," I said. "I'll go away and come back another time."

"Not by a damned sight," he answered. "If all the fools in the country want to go out into the woods and hang themselves instead of taking a club and pounding some sense into their families, it is all right with me. You wait till I get a bite of breakfast and we'll start."

And so we did; we had a very good day, too. The horse stepped along smartly, everyone we met was feeling amiable, and we made several sales. Perhaps we may strike some of you as being hardhearted, but a Yankee will see the agent's point of view: he had a job to do, then was the time to do it, and he wasn't willing to let the ill-considered act of a mad-man upset his plans. And I was Yankee enough to think that he was right.

OVERSOLD

As THE spring wore on it was becoming evident that I had oversold my agents, and it was going to be hard work to make a showing next year in the same territory. Maybe I had overpersuaded them or given them credit for more initiative than they had; anyway, 40 per cent of their stock was still on hand. This was giving me a lot of concern, for I hadn't learned that the things you worry about are never the things that hit you on the head.

As usual, all this worrying was so much lost effort, because late in July the company raised my salary and gave me a new territory. The Vermont man was leaving to work for a competitor, and the firm wanted me to move to Rutland and take over his job. With a great sigh of relief I said good-by to Maine and thought how green the new pasture was going to be, for I was quite sure I could do wonders in Vermont.

When I passed through Worcester on my way to the new assignment and stopped at the office for my list of agents, Mr. Curtis put himself out to entertain me. He told me so many stories about the old days on the road that I had barely enough time to catch my train. Then, when I was grabbing for my hat, he handed me a big bunch of statements and said, "Remember, Gould, we'd rather have you collect a dollar's worth of old bills than sell a dollar's worth of new goods."

He was a shrewd old fellow, for those statements represented about $10,000 worth of old accounts, and if I had examined them before leaving I certainly would have resigned. Someone had been lying down on the job for years, and it was going to be as difficult to get some of these accounts as selling ear muffs in May. I had thought that my territory in Maine was oversold. In Vermont the agents had nearly 75 per cent of their stock on hand!

But there was no use grousing; I snapped out of my gloom and went to work. As collections seemed to be the most immediate job and as Burlington had a lot of agents who owed us money, I took the train for that city. For a week I nosed out our debtors like a hound-dog on the scent of a possum, but didn't collect a cent. When a man has stood off the collector for five years, he seems to think that he has a vested right in the amount and he won't let go.

The last customer I saw was an old deacon who owned a big farm in the neighboring village of Charlotte, but had moved into Burlington and was keeping a boardinghouse. I called him on the phone and learned that he had gone to Charlotte, so I got on the train and tracked him to the farm. He was very pleasant about the matter, and said the bill should have been paid sooner but there was a little error that he was waiting to have straightened out. When I told him I was the man he was looking for, he said all his money was in Burlington and as he was going right back to the city he would see me there. I wanted to ride back with him in his buggy, for I had a hunch I shouldn't let him out of my sight, but he was sorry, he had a lady with him and couldn't take me. However, he promised to meet me at the hotel at noon. I never thought to ask him which noon.

At the hotel I waited—but no deacon; I called the house, but no answer. This was the last straw. I went out on the street and found a hardware store. When the proprietor came up to ask what I wanted I told him that my old boss had always said when he wanted to know anything in a strange town he asked the hardware man, because a hardware man knows enough to handle goods that the rats don't eat and that don't go out of style.

The proprietor gave me a pleased but skeptical look and asked me what I wanted to know. I answered, "The name of the best collection lawyer in town."

He came around the counter, took me by the arm, led me down the street and showed me the building.

"His name is Macomber and you can say that I sent you." He gave me his name, and I went up to the office, which was on the second floor above a dry goods shop. The main office was a noncommittal place, the usual shelves of lawbooks, a table and a few moderately worn leather chairs, not a thing to indicate whether Macomber was old or young, prosperous or merely getting by. A polite young secretary took my name into the private office and came back immediately with the word that I was to go in; no waiting, no effort to impress me.

The man who was sitting behind the desk was as noncommittal as the office, thirty-fivish with a sandy Vandyke and eyes as bright and watchful as a squirrel's. He greeted me adequately but briefly and sat absolutely silent, listening carefully while I told him my story.

To round the matter up I said, "I have done all the talking to these fellows that I intend to do. They have no more idea of paying than a Hottentot has of Sunday. I want you to sue them before the sun goes down."

He answered, "I will do just that."

He got up and shook my hand, and that was all there was to it. I liked the man and went away confident that I had done the right thing and would get somewhere.

At the end of the week, when I returned to the office as Mr. Curtis had instructed, I had plenty to report. The minute he saw me, Mr. Curtis hailed me with, "Hey, Gould, what have you been doing, suing these men? We don't want you to sue people; it isn't our policy."

"It is *mine*," I answered. "When a man owes a bill for five years and won't pay, it is time to do something."

He stuck to it that he didn't want people sued, and we left it at that. He listened to my report on the outlook and told me to go back, work another week, and come in again. The next week as soon as I reached the office the president called, "Hey, Gould, who is this man Macomber?" I said he was the best collection lawyer in Burlington.

"I guess he must be," he replied, "because here is $150, and he says he will have the rest in a few days. Such a thing never happened to us," Mr. Curtis said in an admiring tone. "You'd better give this man some more business."

So I went back and tackled the collections with better hopes; but even so, there were a lot of discouragements. On one trip I had several setbacks in a row and was feeling pretty glum. The company had sent me up to Isle La Motte, which is reached by a seven-mile causeway from the mainland. This was the first time I had ever been out of sight of land in a railroad car, and it gave me quite a start to look out the window and see nothing but water. The trip had been fruitless. I had hung around all day to see an agent who didn't want anything and wouldn't have been good for it if he had, so I went back to the mainland and called on one of our agents who happened to be both the storekeeper and the owner of the village hotel.

The minute I entered the store, he circled around the cracker barrel, keeping it between us as though I were a skunk and he didn't want to have anything to do with me. He didn't have a mower or rake or spreader on display and said he couldn't afford to keep them in stock. I knew the kind,

one of the suspicious fellows who let you know that you can't
get ahead of them. He even demanded that I endorse the company notes that he had cashed so he could get some money
on them. I did know enough to endorse them "without re-
course."

His attitude might not have been so enraging if I hadn't
known that he was one of the biggest dealers in the neighborhood. He owned numerous farms, rented others, and spe-
cialized in pressed hay, which he stored in big barns and sold
in the winter when the snow was hard enough for teams to
haul supplies. Altogether, he was so disagreeable that if there
had been any other place to stay I would have consigned him
to the devil and moved out of the hotel; but there I was,
stuck for the night.

The only bright spot was the man's young nephew from
Boston, who had been spending the summer with the old man.
He was an endlessly curious and active thirteen-year-old who
wanted to be a great trapper and hunter. He told me proudly
that in the spring when he first came he had made some fox
bait that was guaranteed to make a fox leave his family and
friends and run to put his foot in the trap.

Every trapper had his private receipt for fox bait. A local
old-timer gave the boy this one, and he imparted it to me
when I swore that I would keep it a secret forever. The directions called for one cat, one skunk, and one large sucker
(a fish), all to be cut up into small pieces and put in a gallon
jug, the mouth of which should be covered with a piece of
cheesecloth. The whole is put away in a safe place to ripen.
The boy told me his jugful had been ripening ever since early
spring.

Now it was late fall, the first good snow had fallen, and
the old storekeeper was ready for his winter business. That
evening a team drove up, and the driver wanted ten bales of

hay. As all hands were busy, the old man himself went out to the barn to get the hay. The boy and I followed to see what was going on. The barn was packed tight with neat tiers of bales, and it was necessary for the storekeeper to pull out a top one. He was short and could barely get his fingers under it by standing on tiptoe. He inched it along until he could tip it. When he bore down on his end, down came that jug of fox bait. It slid down on the old man's head and exploded like a load of bricks hitting a rotten squash.

You'd have to make up some fox bait and try it yourself to have the faintest idea how that old man stank. I concluded that bait would lure only a feeble-minded fox, for a smart one would have held his nose and run like the devil beating tanbark.

When the storekeeper got his breath, he cursed his relatives, the man who told the boy how to make the fox bait, the boy, the hired men because they hadn't discovered it, and the teamster for laughing. The teamster said he had hauled timber in Maine where cussing is cussing, but he had never heard anything like this. He laughed until he didn't have any breath left, then he went outside and barked like a fox. That started the old man all over again.

The boy and I crept back to the hotel, hoping his uncle hadn't seen us. That night I hid the boy in my room to save him the tanning of his life, and the next morning I left in high spirits. As I drove away from the door I barked like a fox and listened to the storekeeper's curses following me along the street.

Another stop was in Cambridge to see the Cambridge Plow Company. The previous salesman had made a small contract with this firm, and I was instructed to go back and sell them a larger order. The manager seemed to take pleasure in being especially disagreeable. He told me he had no idea of buying anything, but that if anyone wanted a machine he would re-member where to order it. I felt like telling him of a place he could go where his fuel bill would be very small, but I kept still. Getting angry never pays a grocery bill.

That winter I met the man again. He came into the hotel at which I was staying and asked how business was. I told him there wasn't any that I could find.

"Why, you shouldn't be on the road if you can't sell mow-ers," he said. "Mowers are dead easy. If you want to tackle something man-size you ought to try plows. They are the hardest thing there is to sell. and I am getting a nice lot of business."

I could have choked him cheerfully, but instead I went to bed and tossed about all night convinced that I was a failure. The next day the sun was out, and my luck turned.

In one town that I made on this trip I saw an interesting small-time saga of the rise and fall of American business, and if I had been a philosopher it would have given me a lot to think about. The town was actually the property of a family of local magnates who owned the factory, the bank, and a large part of the local real estate. Nearly everyone in the vil-lage worked for them and was dependent on them for bread and butter.

This was the second generation. The father had been a poor boy apprenticed to a local blacksmith. In these mountains where the fields ran up and down the hills, threshing was tedious work, so someone had dreamed up a way of getting horsepower for the threshing machines. His idea was to fur-nish it by horses who climbed up an interminable hill of lags that constantly ran down hill. It was a good idea, but it had one drawback: the lags were forever coming loose from the rollers and no one could devise a way of attaching them securely.

When the power broke down, the blacksmith and his apprentice often had to labor all night. This didn't suit the apprentice, who liked his sleep, so he brooded over the matter until he got the idea of attaching the rollers to the frame instead of the lags. He took out a patent, got backing to put up a factory to make the new horsepower—and so marked a great advance in this method of getting power. The factory was a long way from the railroad, but that wasn't so important then as it is now. From then on the apprentice's fortune was made.

The first time I visited the town the inventor had just died, leaving his children a fine going concern as an inheritance, but over the years I saw everything that the old man had built up slip through their hands. The gasoline engine was just making its appearance, and they evidently did not interpret the effect it would have on their business. This, I thought, was a case in which the father left his money to his heirs and took his brains with him.

I sometimes got my fingers burned while getting used to Vermonters. One agent with whom I was trying to settle an old account and to make a new contract was an innocent-looking old farmer. If you shook him you would have expected to see hayseed drop out of his beard. He told me he didn't think he would handle the line any more, as the mowers didn't stand up. He showed me a mower with the crankshaft almost worn through the frame and said, "I had to take this back." His expression as he looked at it would have touched the heart of Pharaoh. It touched me and made me feel so sorry for him that I promised I'd see him through. I said I'd write the company and make them give him a new frame and on the first holiday I'd come back and put it on for him so he wouldn't be out a cent. The look of what I took to be gratitude in his eyes made me feel proud of my warmheartedness for several days.

On Memorial Day I returned at my own expense, knowing that the company would not look with favor on such a long trip for one call, and put in the new frame. The old farmer beamed with pleasure.

Soon afterward I met the salesman whose territory I had taken, and when I told him about the old fellow, he exploded.

"Why, the old so-and-so," he exclaimed. "He sold that mower to a New Yorker who didn't put any oil on it and burned out the bearing. He admitted it, and we finally took back the mower and allowed him $10 on it toward a new mower. Now the old so-and-so has worked on you so he has a new mower that cost him only $10."

COLLECTIONS

AFTER a few experiences like the one on Memorial Day I was harder to fool; in fact, I was getting such a reputation as a tough bird in making collections that the company sent me to make one in a town on the eastern side of the state. This was most unusual, as it was in another man's territory, but it seemed that this salesman had sold a carload of spreaders to an agent and shipped them to him in August, just before the September fair. At the fair the man saw a new model and fell in love with it. He wanted the company to take his spreaders back and let him have the new ones, and although they couldn't do this, they promised to give him help in selling his. He interpreted this to mean that they would sell the spreaders for him, and every year when the salesman came to settle, he got nothing but a hard-luck story.

Now the account had remained unsettled for three years. The company had given up hope of getting the man who had sold them to act and had sent me to see what I could do. My instructions were to stay until I could get a settlement, and at one time I thought this town was going to be my permanent address.

Having been warned that the man was a wise bird and wasn't likely to give up without a struggle, I took a day to study the land. At the town clerk's office I searched the records but couldn't see a ray of light. The man had effectively prevented legal action by mortgaging everything to his brother, even milk pails and milking stools.

These precautions made me think that it was foolish to threaten. In any case, I preferred to act first and do my threatening afterward; so, as soon as I knew where I stood, I went to see the man. Never have I heard anyone tell so many barefaced lies in such a short time. In addition to the old spreader account, he owed us about $200 for goods shipped that year. I suggested that he pay this bill, as it was overdue, but he said he couldn't pay it just then because he had bought an engine and blower and was going to cut silage for his neighbors as soon as the machinery came. It had taken all his money to make the first payment.

Then I saw a ray of light. The Vermont laws give a seller thirty days to file a claim with the town clerk, and after that the purchase is open to attachment. The machinery had been shipped from a Western city, and according to the law, the blower belonged to the purchaser on the date of shipment. I knew there was no mortgage on record for this, so the next morning I went to the depot and told the freight agent that our agent was complaining about how long it was taking to get his blower, and I would like to know when it was shipped. The agent looked up the date for me, and as luck would have it, the shipment had been made a month earlier. With this information in my pocket, I jumped on the train for Burlington and my friend Macomber. He said that I had done well and that he would attach the blower at once. He asked where he could reach me, and I gave him a list of hotels at which I would stop. So I went on about my business, and two days later, as I was eating my supper in the hotel at Middlebury, I received a phone call from Macomber. He said, "Be in my office tomorrow at ten o'clock if you want to see the maddest man in Vermont."

The minute I entered the office, the agent started to abuse me, but I said, "Hold on, you won't get anywhere with this. You sat and lied to me all the other day and I didn't say a word. You mustn't think I'm as foolish as I look. I had searched the records and I knew all the time just what was the matter with you. You had taken our money and bought a blower and thought we couldn't help ourselves. You see, we can. Now about the four spreaders on hand; they have stayed outdoors until the paint is all off and they are worth about $50. I am going to take them back at that figure instead of the original $100 at which they were billed you. That leaves $200 to be made up. The company has acted very foolishly in this matter, and I am going to fine them one-half. You will have to pay the rest."

When the man saw that he couldn't make me angry, he calmed down immediately. I never could see any sense in getting mad just because the other fellow does. Then in an about-face that took my breath away he said, "That's fair. I will give you $200 today and a note for the rest endorsed by my brother."

Mr. Macomber said that was good. All I had to do was to sell the old spreaders, which was easy, and to tell the company what I had done. They surprised me by answering that this was a better settlement than they had expected and that they were very much pleased with it. What's more, they sent my letter to the other traveling man, and he agreed to pay their loss of $100, so they weren't out a cent.

Another tough assignment that the company gave me was to go up to Craftsbury and get Tom Gallagher to working again. Gallagher had been one of their best agents but he had slowed down, and they didn't know what was the matter.

When I got to the village I learned that the township was damming a river to get cheap water power, which meant that many of the farmers had been flooded out, and Tom Gallagher was making appraisals of the damages. That told me all I needed to know about him, because a Vermonter must have a good deal of confidence in a man to agree to let him evaluate his property.

Going out to the construction job, I found Gallagher, a lank, tall, soft-spoken man who rolled his *r*'s as though he had a sawmill whirring in his throat. He took me around with him in an old mud-spattered buggy, and while he was examining the land that was to be flooded, we talked about the reasons for his slowing down. Gallagher told me what I already knew about our mowers, which, he said, were so bad that he just didn't want to sell them.

Several years earlier, when the mower business was getting away from the Richardson Company because its rivals had improved designs, the brother of the president had attempted to design a new mower that would put everyone else out of business. As a result he dreamed up the most worthless thing ever invented. Since the designer hadn't wanted to admit failure, he wouldn't do anything about them, the local agents wouldn't try to sell them, the Richardson traveling men got discouraged and wouldn't push them, and the company's mower business died a natural death.

"I know more about those old lemons than you do," I told Gallagher, "and it's all bad, but we have had a mower man working out the bugs and now we have a good one. Will you take me to the worst of the old mowers there are around here?"

He agreed, and we went out to a small farm not far from town. When the farmer came out to meet us, I was afraid I was in for a licking. The more he talked about the bad features of the mower, the madder he got, and he seemed to lay all the blame on me. Finally, when he quieted down, I said,

"You have had several years' use of this machine, and now I will tell you what I will do. I am going to ship you a new mower, and when it comes, I will start it for you. If you like it, I will take your old mower off your hands and allow you $20 for it."

He said, "All right," and I sent him a mower. In a week's time I went back and found the mower set up and the farmer still surly. When I asked for a pair of horses, he snapped, "What kind of a team do you want?"

When I replied, "Any kind," he said to the boys, "Hitch up the first two you can catch." They opened the gate into the pasture, and out of about twenty horses they caught an old mare of twenty-seven and a two-year-old colt.

"This is the time I have opened my mouth too far," I thought, as the boys hitched up this ill-assorted pair and started for the field, but I didn't let on. As it turned out, I never saw a better team. We started them in a clover field at one end of which the drainage from the barnyard had produced such a rank growth that it had fallen down and grown up again and was a hopeless-looking sight. When the mower reached this point I yelled, "Whoa," and the team stopped.

The man said, "What did you do that for?"

I told him that a good mower is supposed to cut itself loose without backing up—but I didn't add (although I knew it well) that you have to have a clever pair of horses to do it when the field is high and soggy. If the horses start slowly, the grass will clog the knives. This was the worst place I had seen, but I was putting all my trust in these horses; if the mower cut loose here I thought it would do it anywhere.

The farmer said, "Yes, I know that, but damn it, this ain't giving the mower a fair chance."

As I didn't make any comment, the boy on the mower said, "Giddap," and the little Morgans sprang into the collar and were off. The man was so astonished that he dropped everything, ran to the telephone, and began to ring up his neighbors.

"Bill, come over here and see the damnedest thing you ever saw in your life."

It wasn't any time until a dozen farmers gathered. I had nothing to do but look on. Every time the team came around, the farmer would yell, "Whoa," and when all had agreed it was impossible for the horses to cut the mower loose, he would yell, "Giddap," and they were off; I don't believe any team but those Morgans could have done it, but they went into the collar with such determination that the mower had to go. The farmer was proud of his show and loved that mower as though he had made it himself. You could see that he was going to recommend it to every neighbor he could lay his hands on.

When I shipped in the old mower and wrote the company what I had done and was thinking what a good letter of thanks I would get, I received instead a sharp rebuke telling me not to do this again, as they would not allow any more swaps for these old mowers. I should have known better, for no man likes to admit his errors, and the treasurer was the man responsible for these monstrosities. He would rather lose a good agent any day than pay $20 to correct one of his own mistakes.

I liked Gallagher and stopped to see him whenever I was in that section, although he needed very little help from me. It was not far from Craftsbury that I got caught in a blizzard that winter, one of the worst I had ever experienced, a three-day snow that was piled in drifts by a bitter north wind. You couldn't even stick your head out without getting icicles on your eyelashes. Three traveling men, who had been caught in the village as I was, holed up in the little hotel and filled it to capacity. Luckily the old lady who ran it had a cellar full of hams, jellies, and potatoes.

The last train that came in had been stuck for hours in a drift and didn't try to go any farther. Nobody got off in the village except a young woman and a flock of little children who hung around in the station for a while waiting for the young woman's husband to meet her. He had bought a farm in the neighborhood and had come up in advance to get it ready for the family. After a while, when the agent assured her that nobody could get through the roads in this blow, she saw that she must find some place to stay; so she left the children with the agent and plowed out into the street. First she tried the private homes, because her money was getting low and she didn't know how long she would have to stay; but no one would take her in. It seemed as though everybody in town was full up with people who had been trapped in the storm.

When the woman came into the hotel, we four men were playing a game of pitch around the stove. We heard her ask the old lady for a room and saw her burst into tears when she was told that there wasn't one in the house.

"But what can I do?" she sobbed. "I have four little children, and I must find some place for them. They can't sleep out in the snow."

My partner, a young fellow who sold cream separators, was practically weeping at her pitiful tale. I could see his chivalry rising to the boiling point. He jumped up and invited the woman to take his chair by the stove and dry her soaking shoes. She was pretty, I noticed, with her cheeks flushed and the snow clinging to her yellow hair.

"Now, don't you worry, ma'am," said the gallant young drummer in a voice that was as gooey as buckwheat honey. "We'll find some place for you to stay." The rest of us chimed in; the picture of her and her four little children wandering around in the blizzard was more than we could stand.

While she thawed out by the fire we held a council; if there wasn't any home in town that would take her in, we would have to find one somewhere else. Finally I had an idea: our local agent was the owner of the hardware store, which also carried furniture and practically everything but needles and calico. I knew that he had his warehouse above the store, and he must have plenty of cots and blankets. The rooms would be warm, too, because the pipes from the two stoves ran through it, and we might be able to bring enough pressure to keep the fire going all night.

The boys appointed me to interview the storekeeper, so I pulled my collar up to my ears and started out. At the very first step an icy wind swept my hat into a drift, but I recovered it and got across the street to the hardware store without becoming a case for a Saint Bernard. The storekeeper was sympathetic; he took me upstairs and showed me a pile of cots stacked up against the wall. We cleared a space among the coal scuttles and rocking chairs, set up five cots and covered them with heavy blankets. We had plenty of these and pillows, although there were no sheets. As we went toward the stairs I noticed a row of coffins standing on end.

"The undertaker keeps his stock here too," the storekeeper said, "but probably the young lady never saw one, so she won't be nervous." I hoped not, and never said a word about them when I got back and told her about the plan. She was very grateful and sobbed again into her damp handkerchief.

The separator salesman, who had been doing the entertaining while I was gone, told her to stay in the lobby by the fire while he went for the children. We had invited them to have supper with us before they went to their apartment over the hardware store. She looked so grateful that he went out with a grin on his face as wide as that on a jack-o'-lantern. Presently he came back with the four little children laughing and clinging to his arms, as pretty a flock as you would find in a month of Sundays, a pair of twin boys with chubby faces, and two little girls who looked about the same age but, judging by the superior way in which they talked to the twins, must have been older. We turned the lobby into a menagerie with the bear's den under the old lady's desk. She didn't like that very well, but she was game and after a while produced milk and ginger cookies for the crowd.

Directly after supper we all went over to the hardware store to see that the mother had everything she needed for the night. She blinked her eyes at all the stuff piled around and said they would be very comfortable. The children jumped up and down on the beds and thought so too. I was glad our agent couldn't see them, for he would have suffered for his springs.

Next morning, when the family came over for breakfast, the children were full of the wonderful warehouse; evidently they had investigated every milk can and lawn mower in the place.

"What were the tall boxes standing in a row near the head of the stairs?" the mother asked.

"You mean the coffins?" the separator salesman said without thinking.

"Oh," shrieked the young woman. "I wouldn't have slept a wink all night if I had known what they were." Luckily for her, she didn't need to spend a second night with them. That morning her husband broke through with a team of oxen and bundled his family into a sleigh packed with straw. He was a nice, upstanding young fellow, and we hoped he would get along on the farm. We stood in the doorway and waved them out of sight; then the three of us turned and rent the poor young separator salesman.

"Why in tarnation," we said in one voice, "did you have to tell her they were coffins?"

A DIFFERENT RACE

VERMONTERS are a different race from Maine folk, and it took me a long while to get accustomed to them. The Vermonters who originally came up the Connecticut River were largely of Scottish or Irish descent and were farmers by training and instinct. The down-Easters were anything else. They were descended from lumberjacks, shipbuilders, hunters, fishermen, sailors, maybe pirates, but never farmers, and they never took to farming naturally. Most of them owned a farm, but this was just a place to leave the family while they were engaged in more interesting pursuits. Their differing points of view are well expressed in the old saw that a Vermont farmer sells all he can and eats what he can't sell, while a Maine farmer eats all he can and sells what he can't eat.

Each of these states speaks its own language. If you don't believe me, listen to a little Vermont girl say, "Gertie, see the little bird fly over the church," then ask a Maine girl to say it. The Vermont girl will roll her *r*'s as broadly as any Irishman. She also says "harg" and "darg." The down-Easter, although he has few peculiarities of pronunciation, can be spotted anywhere by his picturesque expressions, most of which are adaptations of seafaring terms. I remember my old aunt, who never went to sea but was as salty as any clipper captain that ever lived, calling to Mother, "This child has got into the molasses and daubed himself from stem to gudgeon," or if it wasn't "from stem to gudgeon" it was "from clew to earing."

When I went back to Maine after learning the ways of Vermont, I used to tell the farmers it would be well worth their time to visit Vermont and see how their neighbors did things. In hauling hay, for instance, the Vermonter spent little time. Each field has a small barn in the center and at haying time a boy with a pair of horses and a long rope straddles the windrow and snakes it down to the barn, where two men pitch it in. By night it is all under cover—and with one-third the work. In winter they turn the cattle out, drive them down to the barn, pitch out the hay on the snow, and let the cows haul it.

Then too, the Maine farmer might learn something from a cheese factory and a hog ranch that I saw operated as a unit. The hog ranch was connected with the cheese factory by a pipe nearly half a mile long, and the hog lot was sown to clover, which was not destroyed, because every hog had a ring in his nose to prevent him from rooting. In the center of the field was a series of immense cement troughs that were filled with scalding-hot whey. The troughs were enclosed with a stout fence and gates that were shut to keep out the hogs until the whey cooled. The whey and the clover made pork very cheaply; I thought it was one of the neatest propositions I had ever seen.

Or consider the arrangement of farm buildings. Maine farmers plan to have everything under one roof, because the snow is so deep in the winter that they want to be able to feed the stock without going out of doors. In Vermont, on the other hand, I have counted as many as thirty-two buildings on one farm. This arrangement is especially good from the point of view of insurance. When the buildings are connected, as in Maine, a fire is bound to be a heavy loss, while in Vermont the loss is often confined to one building.

The Vermont Farmers Mutual Fire Insurance Company has a very low rate. As everyone has his buildings insured in this company, the state trial laws had to be changed in order to get a jury to try a case in court. The law prohibited a man from serving on a jury when he had an interest in the case, and practically everybody was a member of the company.

One characteristic of the Vermonters that I liked was their tenacity. Sometimes as I traveled about the state I caught intimate glimpses of their lives, as a stranger sometimes does. If a man happens to like you, he may give you an insight into his character and history that his close acquaintances never have.

One such man, an agent of ours, I met on a stormy winter day. The snow was blowing and it was bitter cold, so he made me comfortable by the stove. After we had talked a while he invited me to stay to dinner, which I did gladly. After dinner, as we sat by the stove and talked about our childhood, I recalled stories of my boyhood on a rocky Maine farm, and he told me his story. It made a deep impression on me as an example of a man's ability to succeed in spite of handicaps. This man was one of a family of seven children whose father had been a pugilist and had taken good care of them until he was attacked by rheumatism and became a hopeless cripple. Then they were forced to become paupers and were sent to the poor farm.

By the time he was eleven years old this boy became dissatisfied with the institution and ran away. From that moment he made his own living. He went to work for a butcher, driving the cart and peddling meat. One day, when he called at the home of a man who was a member of the overseers of the poor and tried to sell him meat, this man told him that he wasn't going to do business with a "poorhouse deserter."

"That hurt me worse than anything that was ever said to me," my agent said. "I went away resolved that some day I would fix things so he would have to apologize." The boy worked hard and went into business for himself. Eventually he married and settled in the town where he had been a pauper and had driven the butcher's cart. All this time he never forgot the overseer of the poor. When this leading citizen finally put a mortgage on his farm and didn't pay the interest very promptly, the butcher bought it.

"It did me a lot of good," he said, "when that man had to come to the 'poorhouse deserter' to pay his interest."

Finally the man got so far behind that the butcher foreclosed and took the farm.

"But I let the fellow stay until he died, and I got my pay out of the satisfaction of feeling that he was dependent on me for a roof over his head."

I could appreciate his feeling, although I am not sure I would have sheltered the fellow. I have always thought what a terrible revenge this was. However, a man of the caliber of that overseer of the poor would probably die pleased with himself that he had got the best of a hard creditor.

I had a different kind of experience with an agent in a small mountain town near Rutland. It was about eighteen miles over the mountains, so I telephoned to see when he would be at home. He invited me to come over on Sunday and to bring my wife for dinner. On that next Sunday, a beautiful June day, I got a team, and we drove over. We found an agreeable old man in a comfortable farmhouse on a mountainside overlooking a narrow valley. The road the whole length of the farm was lined with immense sugar maples that, the farmer told me, usually yielded a hundred gallons of syrup a year. Those were the days when the farmers from the mountains hauled barrels of maple syrup into town and sold it for seventy-five cents a gallon.

As we sat at dinner we looked out the window and saw a moose in the little garden that was fenced with chicken wire. The farmer's wife threw open the window and shouted at the moose, which jumped out of the garden into the barnyard and then disappeared into the woods.

"I guess he's gone," commented her husband, "but we should have opened the tie-up door and driven him into the barn."

As we sat on the piazza after dinner the farmer pointed to the clouds nearly above our heads and said, "Can you see that house up there? I was born there. At the time of the Civil War my father was drafted and my mother was left alone to raise us five youngsters. We heard from Father right along until the Battle of the Wilderness, and then he was reported missing. Mother took care of the farm and raised us all. I was the youngest, and it was my job every day to walk half a mile down the hill to the mailbox to see if there was a letter from Father. She never gave up hope.

"We all grew up and left the old farm, but Mother wouldn't leave, as she felt that Father might come back and not find her. We all tried to get her to come and live with us, but she wouldn't. Finally we gave up and looked out for her there until she died a few years ago. I bought the old place and shall keep it always."

That was Vermont tenacity for you. I repeated to the old man a story my father had told me about a Vermont regiment at the Battle of the Wilderness. Father belonged to the Sixteenth Maine, which won a reputation as one of the bravest regiments in the Union Army when it held a hill at the Battle of Gettysburg until the rest of the troops could get away. They lost all but twenty-three men in one day.

But Father thought the bravest thing he ever saw was the action of the Vermont regiment that held a position at the Battle of the Wilderness for forty-eight hours before the Sixteenth Maine relieved them. They had been under fire all the time and had repulsed several charges by the best troops the Confederates could send against them, and still they held their ground. They had dug a long grave in the rear of their lines. As fast as a man was killed they laid him in, put up a marker with his name and rank on it, and dug the grave a few feet wider to hold the next casualty. Yet they had held on with this open grave staring them in the face.

The old man sighed, and I could see that he was thinking one of the men in that grave might have been his father. We agreed that this was an example of Vermont tenacity at its best, but it sometimes had undesirable aspects as well. There is no one in the world who can hang onto a dollar with more tenacity than a Vermonter, and sometimes he goes to the most devious lengths to protect it.

For deliberate chicanery I would choose a Vermonter every time, but for plain and fancy lying for the joy of it, I would choose a man from Maine. The down-Easters have it in their blood. When their ancestors returned from far voyages, their stories of adventure excited the admiration of their stay-at-home neighbors, and pretty soon some man whose most exciting moment had been when he was kicked by a cow began to imagine himself as the hero of encounters with savages and wild animals. From thinking about it, he began to talk about it, and soon the state developed a race of tall liars that can't be equaled.

I remember a poster that I came across one day as I was driving along a Vermont country road. It advertised a horse-jockey meet and offered prizes for the man who made the most trades, one for the most worthless horse, and a grand prize for the biggest liar. I wished I could enter a name for that grand prize. It would have been hard to choose from a dozen men I could think of, but if I had to narrow it down to one, it would probably be Alec Marsh, the cook in a lumber camp in Aroostook County. He was not only a great liar but a great cook, and as the camps always fed everyone who came along hungry, Alec's camp was the most popular spot in the big timber. No number of extra guests ever bothered Alec. When someone called that twenty strange lumberjacks were coming up the trail, he would yell to his cookie, "Put a couple of buckets of water in the pea soup."

One night, however, Alec was annoyed. Supper was over, he had gone to bed; and as he had to get up at three o'clock in the morning, he wasn't in the best of humors when three hunters who had lost their way and were hungry turned up for supper. Alec crawled out grumpily and made them such a good supper that they couldn't thank him enough.

"How in the world," they asked him, "can you cook such a grand meal up here in the wilderness?"

"Oh, it's nothing," he assured them. "You should have eaten some of the dinners I cooked when I was out West. I fed 720 Indians every day; but it was easy out there, for I had everything convenient. Right down the middle of the table I had a track. All the cookie had to do was to dump a wheelbarrowload of potatoes and a couple of barbecued beeves on it, and the Indians did the rest. Out back of the cookhouse was a lake of boiling lard. I made doughnuts by the thousand, and pitched them out the window with a hay fork. Then the cookie went out in a canoe and picked them up."

Alec could spin these yarns as fast as he could breathe, and so could old Colonel Sanders, a Maine man who was one of the regular crackerbox sitters in Uncle John's store. One time, I remember, a lumberman from upstate was boasting about the heavy load he carried up the rapids of the Allegash when his boat was grounded on the rocks.

"I grabbed a barrel of molasses under one arm," he boasted, "and a barrel of flour under the other and waded into those rapids, and as I struggled up over the ledges the load was so heavy that my feet sank into the solid rock up to my ankles."

"I don't know that I ever carried such a heavy load," spoke up old Colonel Sanders, "but I doubt if any of you fellows ever carried a bigger one. It was early in the Civil War, when I was just a buck private. The rebels were after us, and we were retreating fast. I was with a detachment guarding the supply train. It had rained for days, and the ground was like soup. In a cut between two hills the wagons stuck in the mud so we had to unload them and carry the supplies on our own shoulders. I drew fifty bass drums, 427 snare drums, and fifteen gross of dippers without handles."

That one was hard to beat, and I doubt if any but a Maine man could do it.

However, I did come upon one Vermonter whom I would back against any of Maine's whopper tellers. He was our agent in a little mountain town where the fields were steep hills and there were many acres of land that couldn't be farmed even by these determined men. This was in the merino section, at that time the center of the merino-breeding industry of the country. The lambs did well in these high mountain valleys and attracted buyers from as far away as the Argentine. It was said that a merino ram would add a pound of wool a head in a flock of sheep, so the prize rams brought top prices, and the whole industry was profitable.

My agent lived on a little farm up on the mountain, where he raised sheep and had a good wood lot and managed to get along. The road was steep, little more than a cart track, so I hoped he would be at home. I asked the first farmer I passed if he happened to know, for I hated to make the trip for nothing.

"I know he's at home," said the farmer. "I have the only wagon there is in the valley, and he can't get away until I come back."

So I drove along until I found the house. The man was in the wood lot, his wife told me, and if I followed the road I would find him. I went along and climbed a mountain until I was sorry that I had ever started. Finally I heard someone swearing, and knew that I was on the right track.

At last I caught sight of two men loading wood on a dray body. The front end was supported on a wood-shod bob-sled, and the sills of the dray dragged on the ground. The hind end was chained to a stump, and on each sill was a bridle chain to drag in the earth and further brake the progress of the outfit when the fid, or wedge, that held it to the stump was knocked out.

I stood and watched the two men pile on wood until they had at least two cords. Then one man climbed on the load, took the reins, and shouted, "All right." The other knocked out the fid that held the chain; the horses sat down in the breeching, and away they slid down that mountain with that enormous load. The bridle chains grubbed in the earth and a great dust arose, but nothing checked the rush of that bob-sled for nearly a quarter of a mile.

When we were safely on the agent's front porch, I mentioned my dislike for such an enterprise, but he said, "We will always take a job fifty cents a cord cheaper on a mountain than on a level, because we can haul so much more."

He acknowledged that it seemed a bit terrifying at first and told me about a French Canadian who worked for him. The first day the Frenchman went up the mountain to yard wood with him, the farmer said when the load was ready, "Get on and drive."

"Not by a damn' sight!" said the Frenchman.

Then the farmer said, "I will drive. You knock out the fid." The Frenchman prepared to release the chains, but first he turned all the way around and said, "Now, Mr. Mountain, you take one damn' good look at this Frenchman, because if you want to see me again you come where I am. I ain't comin' here no more."

"Did he leave?" I asked.

"Oh, no," replied the farmer. "After a while he became accustomed to this country. The other day he was working on the fence when a black cloud came up, one of the sudden storms we have in these mountains when for a few minutes it gets as black as night. After the downpour was over he came into the kitchen to dry off and said to my wife, "I tell you I was scared like hell. I tell you I say my prayers, then when it get light again I get off my knees and say 'To hell with it' and go back to work."

After dinner, when we felt more acquainted, we sat on the veranda and talked about the cost of living. The farmer said he and his large family lived well because they raised nearly everything on the farm. The groceries were taken care of by the butter and eggs. The wool bought the clothing and paid their taxes. They hauled some wood to the doctor and the church to cover those outlays, and the money for the lambs went into the bank. They had the maple-syrup money for extras.

I asked him how much money he counted on each year for extras. He said he needed one dollar to subscribe for the paper and a little for postage and a few things like that. After figuring a few minutes he concluded, "I can get by with seven dollars, but I had ought to have eleven."

As we sat there we looked out on a side hill planted to corn that was in perfect alignment and promised well. I asked him how he got it so even. He squirted a stream of tobacco juice over the rail and answered without batting an eye, "I just sat on the doorstep and shot it in with Dad's old Army rifle." And darned if I didn't almost believe him.

PIRATES

AGAIN I was concerned about my territory, which was loaded up with the previous season's sales. As usual, it was useless to worry. The Teddy Roosevelt panic came along that fall, and there was nothing we could do except to listen sympathetically to the troubles of our agents. I was asked for all sorts of advice, not because my opinion had much value but just because it made some of my agents feel better to express their own. One old customer took me out behind the barn and, after looking carefully around to see that we were not overheard, asked my opinion of the market. I knew nothing that would be of any value, but I ventured to say that I thought the country was sound and it was mostly a banker's panic because Teddy had been shaking the big stick.

"That's just what I think," he answered. "Do you see that smoke over there? That is the Delaware and Hudson Railroad. Every day about this time that train goes by. They are going just the same as usual. The stock always has paid 9 per cent and has sold for 175, and now it is down to 115. I am going to take all the money I have and all that I can borrow and buy D. and H. stock."

I didn't want to say anything for fear of giving the wrong advice, so I kept still, but evidently others felt as he did because it wasn't long before the stock began to advance. I cannot imagine a Maine Yankee doing that sort of thing. He would be more likely to hang onto what he had. They say when a Maine man gets his hands on a dollar, it retires from circulation.

This was the time the company chose to add northern New York to my territory. Although I didn't know it at the time, this was a terrible blow, for the section was as full of consigned stuff as Aroostook.

In addition to the panic there had been a period of poor harvests, and the small farmers were destitute. A traveler for International Harvester, who was also trying to collect old accounts, told me he had several thousand dollars' worth that were on the verge of outlawry and it was necessary to get at least a payment on them to keep them alive for six more years. When he started out his credit man said to him, "Don't take any money with you, or else you will be lending it to these fellows."

That proved to be poor advice, because after he had canvassed all possibilities, the drummer found that the only way he could get payment was to loan the farmer a dollar, then take it back and give him credit on his account or endorse it on his note, and then go on and do the same thing for the next one. Somehow he worked the dollars into his expense account.

"I know you are an honest man and would pay it if you had it," he would say, "so I am going to loan you a dollar, and I know you will pay up when you get a good harvest." He was sure they would, for although these people did a small business they were nearly always within their ability to pay. He was probably right, I thought, but I had never seen such poverty.

Here again was a different country, and I had to learn its ways. When the company sent me to Batavia to help an agent at a fair, I began by asking the farmers who came to our tent how many cows they had, just as I had done in Vermont and Maine. Those who said one or two I passed up as not worthy of consideration. It was some time before I woke up to the fact that the farmer in that section keeps only enough cows to provide milk and butter for his family. After the harvest, when his silo and his cornbins are full and his straw and hay are stacked, he goes down to the stockyard and buys a carload of feeders, say two-year-old steers. He drives them home, opens the door to his shed, drives them in and shuts the door, and that is about all he does.

On the side that faces south the shed is open, and in the center is a watering trough. He feeds the straw and silage, plus a mixture of corn and oats ground together. The cattle run under the shed or stay outdoors as they see fit. In the spring they have gained about 200 pounds each. The farmer then sells them back to the buyer at a profit of about two cents a pound and has no stock to fool with in the summer.

In August, when his harvest is out of the way, the farmer takes his spreader to this yard, loads on it this dry manure, and spreads it over his farm. At least, that is the way he did it forty years ago. We had to work harder to get his business, for with this dry manure he could use Western spreaders. Usually we didn't need to worry too much about their competition, because in New England the manure is wet and strawy as a rule, a condition that our spreader was designed especially to handle. This is why the big Western manufacturers, who knew nothing about our conditions, found some surprises when they came East to get our business.

When he returned from the Dakotas on a visit, the salesman whose job I took over told me that they handled business quite differently in the West. It was his custom to go out selling with a jobber who covered a big district. They would drive out into the country until they came to a crossroads, where there was always a beer parlor in which all the farmers of the neighborhood gathered. All he and the jobber needed to do was to go in and buy the farmers a drink around, then get on with the business. After they had made all the sales possible, they drove on to the next crossroads and repeated the drinks and the sales.

The salesman showed me a picture of a great grass-covered pile of manure around a square foundation.

"That was where the old barn stood," he said. "These mounds are scattered everywhere over the plains. When the farmers threw out so much manure that they couldn't get into the barn doors, they moved the barn." The manure, he said, is old and dry and finely powdered, so the spreaders that handle it are not designed to spread the heavy mess that we must tackle.

Although northern New York was like the West in some respects, it was no different from New England in the matter of collections. The first prospect the company gave me was in Galway, a small town in the bushes not far from Ballston Spa. They had received a glowing letter from a promoter who had a scheme to connect Galway with the outside world by an electric railroad from Ballston. He had bought the country store and hotel and was making a lot of talk about putting Galway on the map. He had spared no adjectives telling the company about the wonderful prospects for business, and he wanted them to send a man over right away to get it. I hadn't been there a day when I began to suspect that the whole scheme was a stock-selling fraud instead of a railroad. The only thing the man had done was to hire about fifty men for half a day and set them to cutting bushes while they had their pictures taken showing work being done on the right of way.

As I had a couple of collections to make in the neighborhood, I wasted no time in Galway. One old pirate had kept a mower on consignment for more than ten years. When I told him that if he didn't want to settle the account I must ship the mower back, he said it was in the barn at his farm and I could drive out and get it if I wanted to. I found only a wheel and an old cutter bar. When he was confronted with these, the old outlaw calmly maintained that it was a sample machine, which he had worn out demonstrating!

Altogether it was a discouraging business. The only pleasant thing about this trip was a boiled dinner that an old lady who ran a little village inn cooked for me.

"You are from Maine," she said the first evening I stopped there. "So am I, and I'll cook you a dinner that will make you think you are at home."

When I came in the next afternoon I sniffed something delicious. I stuck my head in the kitchen door to tell "Grandma" a joke and see what was going on. She called me over to the stove and pointed to a kettle on one of the back holes. In it was simmering a brisket of beef which had been cooking so long that the flesh was ready to drop away from the bones.

"Been on the stove all day," she commented. "Tomorrow you'll have a dinner that *is* a dinner, beef corned in the kettle and everything that goes with it. What do you like cooked in the liquor? Potatoes and turnips, carrots, cabbage, parsnips? And how do you feel about onions?"

I was indifferent about the onions, so she said since I didn't care, she'd put them in.

The next evening Grandma served the beef on a big platter with the vegetables around it. I felt that I ought to tie a spear of grass around my waist like the Australian savages, so I'd stop when the grass broke. The next night we had red-flannel hash colored with the beets Grandma had cooked separately. If domestic-science schools would teach girls how to cook a boiled dinner instead of how to bake a banana, the divorce rate in this country would drop by half.

While I was at Grandma's I went after another bad account in a town near Ballston. A very productive agent of ours had died a few years earlier, leaving nearly $900 due the company. Every time one of our agents tried to collect he was given a sad story by the son, who was the administrator of the estate. He said he had been trying to sell his father's timberland and that he would pay as soon as he could dispose of some of it.

By this time I was of a suspicious nature, so the first thing I did was to go to Ballston, the county seat, and look up the records. It was a shock. The administrator had never filed a list of assets; instead, he had sold nearly everything by giving heirs deeds. It looked to me as though we were licked. I went to a lawyer, who said he had no doubt that was what the son was up to. When he got everything sold off he would file an inventory showing no assets, and we would be out of luck.

He advised me to try to get out an administrator's note. If that was not paid I could sue the bondsmen. I had a note made out in the proper form and got him to sign it as administrator. When it became due and wasn't paid, I went up and read the law to the son and had a check in half an hour. This was the most barefaced attempt at fraud that I had ever met.

After cleaning up this business, I drove on to Saratoga, which at this time was enjoying the height of its popularity as a sporting resort. In the racing season the hotels and restaurants did a land-office business. Along the road I noticed great flocks of guinea fowl and wondered what was the market for all of them. My driver told me that they were sold to the hotels. As they had dark meat like that of game birds, when they were about half grown the hotels were able to pass them off as woodcock at $5 apiece. The raising of guinea fowl and the sale of Epsom salts to dope the water of the mineral springs were lucrative businesses.

As we pulled up at the Commercial House, which, as its name indicates, was the drummer's home, a slippery-looking duck accosted me and asked for a quarter to get a cup of coffee and something to eat. As he looked able-bodied, I said, "I'll do a lot better than that for you; I'll get you a job."

"What doing?" he asked warily.

"Husking corn. I saw a man yesterday who wants a man to husk ten acres, and he will pay five cents a bushel. You can make good pay."

"I don't know if I would like it," he said, and I didn't either, but that was as far as I was going. Saratoga was the hangout of such fellows. It was at about this time that Governor Hughes was making his fight against the racing bill. He won and put an awful crimp in this crowd, some of whom had to go to work whether they liked it or not.

The night of the election I was in the Commercial House. The old German who ran it had sunk his entire capital in the lease of the hotel, expecting business to continue, and he was very bitter against Hughes. To the last he believed that racing would win.

As a crowd of us sat around the stove waiting for the returns, a couple of old-timers swapped tales about the days of marching clubs and torchlight parades, when politics was fun. One of them, a down-Easter, told about an incident in the Cleveland-Harrison campaign when his club set out for Dover in a special train paid for by the local candidates. When these celebrating Republicans pulled into Dover, they were met by a Democratic club chanting a catchy ditty that the visiting

Republicans promptly stole and changed to extol the virtues of Harrison. The Democratic version was as follows:

> Ladies and gents, ladies and gents,
> The Democratic party is surely immense.
> Hoo-Rah, Hoo-Rah, Cleveland, Cleveland!
> Rah! Rah! Rah!

Not to be outdone, the Democrats put on a parade of their own to boost the fortunes of Frank Jones, a Portsmouth brewer who was running for Congress. As they marched down the main street, they were delighted to see the jail brilliantly lighted and they broke into cheers, forgetting in their beery state that the local officials were solidly Republican. Their enthusiasm promptly fizzled out when they looked a second time. Every window of the jail was crowded with the heads of inmates and over them stretched a transparency that read,

JONES'S BEER PUT US HERE.

I could match their stories, for while I was working for Uncle John I got both business and political training in a campaign club. We were the last word in campaigners with our silk hats, long white coats, canes, and red hoods hanging down our backs, and we paraded behind an express wagon carrying a calcium light that was turned on us and designed to put all other clubs in the shade.

Our reblocked silk hats cost $1.50 apiece and our coats and canes $5. I did a little figuring and announced in meeting that I could furnish the hats for $1 and the coats and canes for $3.75. In my innocence I didn't realize that I was breaking up a very neat little graft that had been held for a long time by a firm of old contractors. Uncle John was so pleased that he acted as though I had won the election singlehanded.

Uncle John was the greatest artist in political matters that I ever knew. On stormy evenings when trade was quiet, he used to tell us about his exploits. During the Civil War he lived in Portsmouth, which was strictly Republican, as all the businessmen were getting rich on government contracts and the voters in the Navy Yard and private shipyards were compelled to vote the Republican ticket under threat of losing their jobs.

But the Republicans weren't smart enough to get ahead of Uncle John, who mapped out the Democratic campaign. The ballots in those days were enormous sheets of paper. The Republican ballots were identified by an oversized American eagle printed on their backs, making them so conspicuous that it looked impossible for a sneaking Democrat to vote an opposition ballot without being caught.

That was where Uncle John exercised his genius. He had the Democratic ballots printed on small pieces of tissue paper, and this was the way he slipped them into the ballot box: His Democrats approached a certain heeler who was passing out Republican ballots at the voting hall. Soon the heeler left his post to go to the toilet, where he passed his bunch of Republican ballots to an accomplice who took them into a barroom down the alley and pasted Democratic ballots over the names of the Republican candidates. On the next trip of the heeler these were exchanged for another lot, and in no time all the heelers were loaded with the bogus ballots.

The bosses who watched the stream of eagles going into the ballot box were ready to swear that they had carried the city by 10 to 1. They were mad enough to bite a hornet when they found that they had lost, but not so mad that they couldn't appreciate genius when they saw it. The next year Uncle John led the Republicans to victory.

Even the disconsolate old proprietor laughed at the contrivances of Uncle John, but when the returns began to come in at about midnight and it was evident that Hughes had won and he was ruined, he slumped behind his desk in abject despair. We felt so sorry for him that we started a run on the bar and gave it the best business it had ever had.

ALONG THE BORDER

ORTHERN New York was the toughest assignment I ever had. Mooers Forks, the Ellenburgs, Cherubusco, Chateaugay, all seemed to me to have been made only to keep the world from unraveling. So did the country around Dannemora. As I watched the prisoners from the state penitentiary walking around the streets, I wondered why they didn't try to escape, but after a while I decided that they knew they were better off inside than out.

The northeast corner chamber of the little inn at Cherubusco was the coldest spot I had ever encountered. To make matters worse, the innkeeper was on a drunk and his wife was having hysterics. There was nothing to eat for supper but a few cold doughnuts, not even a cup of hot coffee, but there was no reduction of the rate on that account. To suffer from indigestion in a stone-cold room with the wind howling down from the north and the temperature below zero is one of those experiences that raise gooseflesh on your spirit even when you think about it years afterward. In addition to these discomforts collections were bad; if one came easily it was such a surprise that I was sure something must be wrong.

Along the border the population was largely French, little villages with whitewashed hewn-log houses that looked as if they had stood there a hundred years or more around a church that represented more money than all the town put together.

From one of these villages I drove out to his farm to see

our agent and found him threshing with a full crew of girls, all his daughters. It was a dirty job, but the girls were doing it well and seemed to regard it as just part of the year's work.

The agent said he would go out with me to see a prospect, so he went into the house to get his gun in case we flushed some game along the way. He brought out one of those old discarded rifles of the Mexican War that hung in three out of five Maine kitchens when I was a boy and that carried a bullet about the size of a croquet ball. The old contraption brought back sharp memories of the first time I ever tried to shoot one.

The event that led up to the episode which, my father always maintained, accounts for my being a runt in a family of tall men, was the bean-pulling bee of our neighbor the deacon. In those days any man who raised seven bushels of yellow-eyed beans in one year was entitled to be addressed as "deacon." This man was undoubtedly a deacon, as he raised a lot of beans, but when harvest time came his bean bee was not a success.

Usually we liked these bees, for after the young men and boys had pulled and stacked beans all afternoon while the girls looked on, the harvester entertained with a supper and a dance, or as near one as his convictions would allow. This man must have had a lot of convictions. As one of the boys expressed the general sentiment, he would be damned if he would stand on his head all afternoon for the old skinflint and get nothing for it but a drink of lemonade and a dough-nut.

As I was only twelve years old and this was the first invitation anyone had bothered to give me, I showed up early. Nobody else came, but I labored diligently and at the end of the afternoon was rewarded with a quarter.

It seemed to me that the heavens had opened and showered

me with riches. On several occasions I had possessed a cent, sometimes two, once I had owned five, but a whole quarter! Father, I knew, would invest it for me, but I had my own ideas, so I broke the world's running record to Tinker John's hardware store and came home with a quarter pound of powder, half a pound of number 4 shot, and a dozen caps concealed about my person.

Being eager to see whether the caps would explode, I placed one unostentatiously behind the frying pan in which Mother was cooking potatoes for supper. It worked! Mother jumped and screamed; so did my brother, in whose chin a fragment of copper lodged. Father jumped and I screamed as he held me off the floor by one ear and demanded where I got that cap. For days I was reminded of my crime by my brother, who resisted all attempts to remove the copper that turned his chin a beautiful green and made him the admiration of his schoolmates.

After the explosion, time dragged its feet until Father and Mother went to the quarterly meeting at South Lewiston and gave me an opportunity to try out our old gun. This one, which hung on a couple of crotches in our summer kitchen, had a wooden stock that ran the whole length of the barrel. On this stock were cut many notches, which, according to my uncle, represented rebels that Father had killed in the Civil War. I imagined long lines of dead men and my father walking down the line, stopping at each man long enough to cut a notch. Later I discovered that the notches stood for woodchucks that my uncle had killed.

As soon as the old mare had carried Father and Mother past the schoolhouse, I got my ammunition, took down the gun, and went out behind the barn to load. I couldn't reach the muzzle, but managed it by climbing up on the oxcart. From an old powder horn I poured what looked like a generous portion of powder into the gun, then stuck in about half of the Lewiston *Journal* and rammed it down for wadding. Next I poured from my bottle of shot what seemed to me like a grown person's dose and put that in, also what remained of the *Journal*, all rammed down with the old iron ramrod. When the ramrod stuck out of the barrel about fifteen inches, I decided that the load was enough.

Down the lane beyond the pasture bars I saw a fox smelling around a stone pile. I squatted, rested my gun on the bars, and took careful aim. As I was about to pull the trigger it occurred to me that he was rather far away, so I called him by chirping like a mouse. The fox came toward me; I waited until he was about thirty yards away, then pulled the trigger. A muffled click was the only result—I had forgotten to put on a cap. The fox changed ends rapidly and in a minute had passed out of my life.

Comforted by a few words that I had heard used in such circumstances, I remedied the defect in my artillery and went on. All day I toted that cannon and never even saw so much as a red squirrel.

About four o'clock in the afternoon, as I was creeping along a sheep path in a thicket of firs, a shadow swept over me and a crow alighted in a dead ash tree directly over my head. Noiselessly I raised the gun, rested it on the top of my shoulder, and pulled the trigger. There was a frightful explosion, and something hit me a blow on the shoulder that literally knocked me out. When I came to, the crow—or what was left of him—lay near me. Wearily I dragged my feet home, hung up the gun, and went to picking up rocks. When Father came home and saw my lame shoulder he weakened for once and said I had been punished enough.

Be that as it may, I regarded the agent's gun with no joyful anticipation and planned to be as far away as possible when he decided to shoot. As we drove along I kept his attention focused on spreaders as much as I could, and luckily we didn't come across any game.

In this country I saw evidence of a curious and little-known episode in our history. Not long after the Civil War a group of Irish Fenians started to invade Canada, one group setting out from Malone, another from Calais, Maine. They were well financed and had managed to collect a fairly large stock of arms and munitions from the Army supplies closed out after the Civil War. When they had marched as far as Fort Covington, they were halted and disarmed by our troops. Eventually the supplies were loaded in wagons and sent back to Malone, but the teamsters made a pleasure trip of the return. They stopped at every farmhouse and gave the family a pair of blankets, a gun, and some ammunition. By the time they reached Malone there were no munitions left with which to start another invasion.

As we were near the Canadian line, we did business with a few Canadians. One day when I was out with the local agent we halted a Canadian atop a wagonful of oats and tried to make a deal with him, but he didn't want to talk. He said, "I'll see you as soon as I unload." The agent explained to me that the man had a load of smuggled oats and wanted to get rid of them as soon as possible. He had hauled them down the back streets to avoid passing the customhouse. The customs officials didn't say anything to a man who was bringing over a load of his own oats if he kept out of sight, but they got after those who tried to buy oats and sell them across the line.

A few blocks farther we came upon a store that sat directly on the line—one half in Canada and the other in the United States. The goods that were in the greatest demand on the other side were piled up on that side, but where they could be moved over the line with little effort. Not much was being done to stop the traffic, and everyone seemed happy.

In a little hotel in one of these villages I found a crowd of drummers all having a hard time getting business. As we sat at a big table for supper we told our experiences. One man said, "I got two orders today. One customer told me to get out and another told me to stay out."

After we had all made the best story we could out of our hard luck, someone asked an old man who had been sitting there and saying nothing, "How are things with you, Pop?"

The old man answered cheerfully, "Why, not too bad, but that isn't strange, because they arrest men who don't buy my goods."

After a moment's silence someone asked, "What do you sell?" and he solemnly answered, "Men's pants."

In this section I found that although the mower business had been loosely conducted, the binder business was worse. One of the stock stories the implement salesmen liked to tell was about the man who went to his neighbor's house and found him crying. He had been to town trying to get someone to trust him for enough twine to bind forty acres of wheat, and no one would do it.

"You don't know how to manage. Just come with me and I'll show you," said the friend. They went to town and the friend said to the hardware merchants, "Bill wants to buy a binder."

He was shown a new binder to be paid for in three annual payments. Then the friend said, "You'll throw in enough twine to bind his grain?" The agent answered "Yes" quite cheerfully.

The reason for this state of affairs was that the binder firms were willing to take a farmer's notes, and the dealer had no interest in them. He turned over enough to pay the wholesale cost, and the rest was velvet.

Now that the mower business was tightening up, I had to sell mowers to be paid for the following November, or if they remained unsold, the agent could carry them over for one year without interest by signing a note. Even this was called pretty tough treatment by some agents.

These carry-over notes were a boon to the small agent, but they were a nuisance to the salesman, and whenever we implement men got together we grouched about them. One day I was unloading my woes on a rival about the antics of an old agent who was always asking for allowances, five dollars for going somewhere to make a repair or trying to make it, a dollar for this and another for that. The other salesman looked surprised.

"Oh, I don't have any trouble with that kind," he told me. "I always allow what the fellow asks and charge it off on the carry-over note."

I saw the light, and after that I always followed his policy. The farmer paid that much more cash when I collected, feeling that he was getting his allowance, and the company lost nothing. Everybody was happy.

The majority of farmers weren't very acute businessmen. Another account that I was sent to collect in Plattsburg was an example of the way they let things slide if no pressure was put on them. This account had been standing for three years, and the man was good for it. He came in town to see me, and when I told him my business he began to say how hard times were and how he had ten gallons of maple syrup on his wagon that he was taking home because he couldn't get anyone to buy it. After I explained that we had trusted him for three years and couldn't do it any longer,

I suggested that he go over to the bank and tell them that he owed us and wanted to borrow $200 to pay the debt.

"I never borrowed any money at the bank in my life," he protested.

"Now is a good time to begin," I assured him. After much persuasion he went over, although it took all the courage he had. In ten minutes he came back, his face covered with amazement, and said, "What do you think? They let me have it right off!"

It was in this same district, in the little town of Chazy, that I achieved the luxury of my first coonskin coat. In those days everyone who drove in winter owned a fur coat which, whether it was a humble goatskin or an aristocratic raccoon, was the label of its owner's prosperity. Only the most wealthy could afford a coonskin because these coats sold at from $100 to $150, a lot of money in those days.

Our agent in Chazy who dealt in farm implements, carriages, harness, robes, and fur coats had expanded, taken in a partner, and opened a branch in Plattsburg. Unluckily the young partner liked a drink once, or more often twice, in a while. When I arrived in town the firm was overloaded with fur coats for fair; a drummer had plied the young partner with liquor and sold him a carload of them. Among these coats were a number of coonskins, so the agent offered to sell me an unusually handsome one for $80. My old coat was worn bare, but I didn't think I could afford to pay such a sum and turned down the proposition.

That Sunday when I was at home going over the week's events with my wife, I told her about the coat. Immediately she demanded that I buy it and thus demonstrate my affluence; she thought it would help me in my business. So I was persuaded. I wrote a check for $50 and mailed it to the agent with a letter saying that if he wanted the check more than he did the coat, it was a sale.

I wore that coonskin for years and made people think I could afford a $150 coat; but to this day I sometimes feel a pang of regret that I took advantage of a firm's necessity.

SECONDHAND SPREADER

W HEN the firm sent me a telegram to report to the office immediately and offered me Connecticut, I was suspicious. This always had been the best territory, and they kept their top men there, so I was afraid they might have some unusually tough job on hand for me.

However, this wasn't the case. The office was in a turmoil, and old Mr. Curtis and the sales manager were sizzling with indignation. Their Connecticut agent had taken to drinking and had been warned repeatedly, but in spite of all his promises he had committed the unpardonable sin of going on a bender at the Danbury Fair. All day he had lain under the exhibit in a stupor and in the evening he had picked up a lady friend and staged a battle with her that landed him in jail. The whole story was in the papers, and some kind friend had mailed a copy to the office. The agent had been recalled and banished to a remote corner of Massachusetts.

The sales manager said I could have the territory if I could manage it, warning me that the former agent was a very popular man and that any criticism of him would be out of place. This seemed like a real gift of Providence. I cleaned up my business in Vermont and left for Hartford.

The city was unfamiliar to me. Arriving at night, I saw an illuminated hotel sign near the station and went over to ask for a room. The clerk gave me a peculiar look but he let me have one, although obviously I wasn't the kind of guest he was expecting. When I saw the room I understood why. It had been occupied recently; the only furniture was a folding bed, a table, and two chairs, and the table was covered with rings from the bottoms of wet glasses. The sounds I heard indicated that the hostelry was full, but, trusting in the Lord and the fact that a Maine Yankee doesn't give up his money without a struggle, I went to sleep and was not bothered.

In the morning when I went to the post office and asked to be assigned a box, an old woman who had a face like a very dull meat ax took up a blank and demanded my address. I told her I didn't have one, as I had just landed in town the night before.

"Where did you stay last night?" she snapped. When I named the hotel, she glared at me as though I were a menace to the community. I ventured the remark that I wasn't going to stay there again, and she shook her head.

"I should say not."

After registering at a good drummers' hotel I began to look around. The makers of the Fearless spreader, I soon learned, had an aggressive agent in Hartford, and he was getting all the business. It was my job to break into his monopoly, but how? As I visited our agents in the little villages around Hartford I kept my ears pointed, and almost at once I heard of a man in the near-by town of Cromwell who was dissatisfied with his Fearless spreader. Within the next day or two I went out to call on him. The man was a Dane who owned a large greenhouse, grew roses, and shipped them throughout the country. He kept a big dairy herd, mostly for the manure, which he threw into big cement tanks and soaked with water that he drew off and pumped on his roses. The residue was pretty solid stuff, and his spreader couldn't handle it.

The agent instead of taking out the spreader had pocketed his money and made no effort to look after the machine, so the Dane sputtered with indignation every time he spoke of it. He was down not only on the Fearless but on all spreaders, and it took a lot of talk to get that pugnacious look out of his eyes and to persuade him to let me put in one of our Worcester Kemps on trial. I was not so sure myself that it would make good, for that manure was almost as hard as sheetrock; but it did, and the Dane was only too glad to swap the Fearless for it.

With the old machine on my hands I put an ad in the paper, "Fearless spreader, good as new, $50." Every man who had thought of buying a Fearless answered it, and all I had to do was to tell them that this spreader had been sold to the owner of the greenhouse but that as it couldn't do the work, I had swapped him a Worcester Kemp for it. It was just as good as new; it hadn't spread ten loads and was a wonderful trade. The more I praised that spreader, the surer the would-be buyers were that it was no good. Every word of praise I said about it put a crimp in the Fearless business.

That winter I put in an exhibit at an agricultural exhibition and met a lot of farmers, among whom I got some good agents. One, a young man from Putnam, at first made very little impression on me, but when he pulled out his checkbook and wanted to pay for his contract, I changed my mind. He said he had some prospects that ought to be seen at once, so I went over to help him. It was early spring and the snow was still on the ground, but the air was soft enough to promise a thaw. As we rolled along behind a beautifully matched pair of bays, I noticed a red fox running across an open hillside. Instead of keeping on in a straight line it went off at an angle to the edge of a little patch of woods, they returned to its course. The young man saw me watching.

"He's scenting a woodchuck's hole. This country is full of foxes, and they are the cleverest animals you ever saw. They have it figured out so if they are cut off from their dens they'll always have an emergency hide-out. After every snow they go around and scent the woodchuck holes so they can find them in a hurry. It snowed a little yesterday," the agent said, "enough to cover up the scent, so this morning we may see two or three foxes out marking them again. Do you want to see?" he asked. Twisting the lines around the whip, he climbed out of the buggy, and I followed. We crunched across the field. When we reached the spot where the fox had stopped, he felt around with his foot until he found the hole. He sank in it halfway to his knee.

The young man read the woods and the fields along the road like a textbook. Every track in the snow, every damp streak on the bark of a tree gave him information about the approach of spring. As a matter of fact, he himself had the alertness and the grace of a woods creature; you felt he ought to be dressed in skins and moccasins instead of in store clothes and a hard hat.

Although I knew the woods lore that every farm boy learns, I could not match him. The best I could do was to tell him about the fox Father trapped once and kept in a dog kennel in the back yard. For a while the wily creature lived handsomely. When Father fed him he left some of his food spread out in front of his kennel, then lay down to wait until the foolish chickens came around to get it. While they were pecking away, he marked a fat young one and sprang out on it. He had chicken for dinner every day until Mother put her foot down.

Presently we drove up to the gate of a prosperous-looking little farmhouse. "The old fellow here has one of the first spreaders your company ever made and he needs a new one.

He can afford it, too, but it's hard to part him from a nickel," the agent said.

The farmer was pleasant enough, but he couldn't see anything except a swap. The company wouldn't do this, I knew, so it took me a long time to talk him into buying a new spreader outright and letting me sell this one for him.

When the old farmer finally agreed, I wrote an ad offering the old spreader for sale and put it in the Norwich *Bulletin*. It turned out to be the best move I ever made. When I reached Norwich a few days later, it took me two hours to read the pile of letters from people who wanted to buy a spreader, and I saw that I had found the best way to uncover prospects that I ever heard of. As there were few agents in this section, all I had to do was to follow up these prospects. For a time I was high man; every day I turned in sales, and the company tried to find out how I did it.

One day I drove out to see a prospect in North Stonington and found a large farm and a barn at least 150 feet long, with every cellar door bursting with the pressure of manure. This was no place for an old secondhand spreader, but as the farmer had answered the ad, I opened up about it. As soon as he found out how old it was, the tough old Yankee stopped me with "Hell, I don't want that thing."

With this I heartily agreed.

"Here is what you want." I took a photograph of the new Worcester Kemp out of my case and showed it to him. By this time I had persuaded the company that good photographs made far more sales than folders or catalogues. "I couldn't tell until I saw you, but you want a modern machine —and this is the one for you."

"How much?" he asked, and when I told him the price, "You ask too much."

"How do you know?" I countered. "You don't know what

it costs to make one. If you name your price, someone is likely to make you an article to fit it—and leave out something you need. Now if you give up the idea of price and think about days' work there isn't anything to do but buy this one. We are the oldest firm in the business and if the machine goes wrong you can go to your phone and within an hour you will have a man who knows how to fix it."

As I started to make out an order, he said, "What are you doing? I ain't going to buy a spreader."

"Of course you are," I told him. "You may not buy it of me, but you are not foolish enough to try to handle that cellarful of manure without a spreader, and you might as well buy it of me as anyone."

I finished the order and handed it to him with a pen. He read it all through, signed it and said, "How in hell could you sell me a spreader in fifteen minutes? Your company has sent a man down to see me every year for five years and the last one said he was going to stay until he sold me. I told him he had better write the company that his address would be North Stonington. How did you do it? How many have you sold this way from that ad?"

"This makes eighteen, and the reason the others didn't sell you, I guess, was that they went to arguing, and you got mad. I have just told you."

"That was just it," he answered, bursting into a laugh. "Now *I'll* tell *you* where to go and sell another."

He sent his son to show me a short cut through the woods to his brother-in-law's place. This farmer told me I was too late; he had bought a Fearless just the day before. The salesman who sold it to him, I learned, was my predecessor, who had returned from his banishment in Massachusetts and gone to work for our rival, so I knew I was up against some dirty work.

"You have bought one of the best, and you are going to like it," I commented. "It is well made, with an easy draft, and is a good job."

The farmer looked at me a minute and said, "That isn't the way the agent talked about yours."

"He ought to know; he has sold both," I answered guardedly.

According to his story our machine had driven him off the road, the farmer told me, and he had gone to work for the Fearless people. That wasn't the way I had heard it, I said, but perhaps I was wrong. The farmer dropped his voice and asked, "Isn't he a man who drinks sometimes?"

"Well," I hesitated, "I would say he was a man who is sometimes sober."

He chuckled and asked, "Where can I reach you if I want you?" I gave him the phone number of the office in Worcester and went on without thinking too much about him, because there seemed to be very little chance of getting any business out of him then. Three days later, as I came into the Atlantic House in Bridgeport, the clerk told me the office had been calling me all day. When I got the sales manager, he said a man in Stonington wanted to buy a car of mowers and asked me if he was good for it. I assured him that the man was, but when he wanted to know how I got such a good prospect, I didn't tell him.

Another situation in which I had to use my wits was the one I found at Windsor Locks. One of the first agents the company asked me to see was a firm there, a large account that would have to be handled very carefully. I was careful for some time but wasn't getting anywhere; the firm was sitting on the best territory in the state and giving all its business to the International company, and we were letting them get away with it. At last I decided on drastic action.

I went out to a small village about five miles away, made a small contract, and sent the man a mower and a rake. He set them up, and in a day or two I got a letter from the company that almost singed my hair.

According to the company I had pulled down the foundations of the temple; I must see the agents at once and repair the damage. It was pretty discouraging; all my good moves turned out to be, if not contrary to orders, at least opposed to the company's policy. I went to see the firm, but instead of apologizing I said, "I am sent down here to get some business for my firm. I find you in one of the best territories we have, giving all your business to the other fellow. Now I want to give you this business, but I can't as things are now. Why don't you come into the ark and be saved?"

One of the partners looked at me a minute and asked, "What do you want?" I told him I wanted to ride with his man a week and see if we couldn't get some spreader business started. He agreed, and we were off.

Before we had gone very far we had sold a carload of seven, and the company had shipped me two more. As luck would have it, this was just before the Hartford Fair, so it occurred to me what a splendid exhibition they would make, all nine instead of the usual one. The company shipped them to me at the fair, and while I was setting them up the other spreader men came around and asked what I was trying to do.

"You don't understand psychology," I told them. "You come here with one, and people think it is a side line. We come here with a lot, and they will buy ours every time, just from sheer power of suggestion."

"Like hell they will!" they said, but I could see that they were a bit nervous and I was determined to show them. I bought several big pieces of cardboard and a brush, and every little while I would paint a sign and tack it on a spreader, "Sold to Henry Skinner of East Hartford," or any one of the other names to whom it actually had been sold. I followed up with about two a day and drove the other agents almost crazy. We sold two extra machines and nailed down the spreader business so that it was almost impossible for any other agent to spin a thread.

My newly converted agents wanted me to help them at the Suffield Fair, but as it came the week of the Danbury Fair, I asked the company to send another man. Together, they sold ten spreaders. The other man said to the sales manager when he got back, "You are always telling me what Gould is doing down in Connecticut, but look at the agents he has. If I had such agents, I could sell goods."

"Gould got this firm," the sales manager told him. "Why don't you get some like them?" This wasn't the truth, as the company had the firm as agents when I went there, but I did train them. They made the largest sales of any retail firm the company ever had.

But being just a little bit smarter than the other fellow wasn't the only way or even the best way to get sales. You had to really think about your agent's problems, even the problems of the community, and help solve them. What helps other people helps you.

Take the matter of the grange hall in North Stonington. My agent was also the master of the grange, and as I was a member, we often talked about grange matters. One of his chief concerns was the mortgage on the hall, and he was anxious to pay it off. If I could think of some way of helping him do this I would not only be doing my agent a good turn and helping the community but I would also be building up good will that would pay off in future business. My suggestion for lifting the mortgage was a grange fair; but my agent was doubtful about this idea, as the town had no grounds and no building. That didn't matter, I argued; they could show cattle in a field and the fancywork and fruit in the grange hall. If they would plan to hold it after the big fairs were over, I'd try to get the company to send me down one of the big display tents that we used to house our exhibitions at the state fairs. I would show outdoors and let them have the tent for the poultry show.

The members of the grange all went to work and put on a show that would be hard to beat. They had big crowds from Norwich and Westerly and cleared about a thousand dollars.

I did a pretty good business, too. There was money in Connecticut, and I was just beginning to get used to it. After having been accustomed to a trade that paid off with farmers' notes, a little cash, and a carry-over note, it gave me a queer feeling to see these Connecticut farmers reach for a checkbook and write a check for the whole amount.

ONE-LUNGER

AFTER working Connecticut a few months I saw the advantage of traveling in an automobile. It would get me around faster; even more important, it would confer on me a certain prestige, as I would be the first implement man in the state to have a car. The company was willing to allow me a fixed amount per day for the use of the car and to pay for gas and oil, so I began to look around. I answered an advertisement of a man in Webster, Mass., who had a Maxwell to sell; and after dickering with him a while, I bought it, with the proviso that he teach me to drive. Though only a one-lunger, it was a very highly regarded car in those days.

There were no road tests, no licenses required; I simply went over one Sunday to get the car, and after the owner had watched me drive about a mile and had pronounced me a driver, I said good-by and set my compass course for Hartford. For about twenty miles all went well. Then, as I was climbing a steep hill, a man came out of a house, shouting in an authoritative voice, "Hold on there! Hold on!"

Afraid I had violated a traffic law, I put on the brake and stalled. As the car had no hand brake, all I could do was to sit there on the hill and hold it with the foot brake. While I was pressing it down until my foot cramped, the man arrived at the car and thrust at me a little framed appeal that said, "The bearer is a poor cripple and would appreciate any assistance you can give him."

151

With all the blistering epithets that I could think of, I assured him that he wasn't half the cripple he would be if he ever stopped me again.

Cussing was some relief to my feelings, but it didn't get the car started. As I couldn't hold it with the brake and get out and crank it at the same time, I didn't know what to do. At last, as my foot was giving out entirely, I let the Maxwell run backward down the long hill. At the bottom I got out and cranked.

But the car was a great help. Agents who were too busy to ride with me when I was driving a horse and buggy always took time to go out in the car, although often it took us longer than it would have if we had stuck to the horse. The pins that held the universal joint were always coming loose, and we spent a lot of time looking for them along the road. The frame was weak too. One side cracked, and the garage in Hartford that fixed it for me charged $25. A few days later, when I was out in the country, the other side cracked. Luckily it happened a few yards from a blacksmith's shop, so my passenger and I loafed around town waiting for the smith to finish shoeing his horses. When he finally got around to it, he charged me $2.60.

By this time my wife was so accustomed to the antics of the Maxwell that she never expected me until she saw me, but I often worried about the anxiety the wives of my agents must have been suffering. Most of the men themselves, however, put our experiences down to adventure and probably made good stories out of them when they got home.

One day when an agent was with me, we went to call on the owner of a stock farm not far from Hartford. The agent knew the way and directed me, but when we approached the farm, he waited too late to say, "Turn here."

As I swung sharply into the drive, both front tires burst. In those days we carried our own repair kits, so there was nothing for me to do but jack up the Maxwell and start to mend the tires. For half a day we blocked that farmer's driveway. He came in from the barns, a houseful of children gathered around to watch, and even the hired men dawdled as they went back and forth to the kitchen. The farmer said he was going to send me a bill for the loss of a half day's work, but he gave us a good dinner and bought a rake and a mower. He could have written off their cost as entertainment, for I never had a better audience.

All this time I was working down through the list of agents that the company had given me. It was an exhaustive list with not only names and volumes of business but also notes on the capabilities of the various men, estimates that sometimes did not agree with mine.

In one little town we had a very capable agent who, the company told me, was doing so well that I need not go to see him until it was convenient. As I was busy, I didn't get around to it until I picked up the paper one morning and noted that he had died. As soon as possible I stopped in the town to find a man to take his place. This is the hardest job there is. When you have had no one almost anyone will be an improvement, but to fill the shoes of a good man is difficult. I spent the day and found a man who was financially responsible, but, as is often the case, he wasn't interested; so I gave up the attempt and decided to wait and see if I couldn't find a lead.

Sure enough, one day at the Danbury Fair this same man who had refused the agency came around and told me that he had a boy of seventeen who was going to high school in Shelton and thought he could sell some tools to the farmers at night and in the mornings. The father said he would help the boy, but he wouldn't buy very much. As it was about my only hope, I wrote a contract with him for a small amount and felt that I had done as well as I could; still, it was going to be short of what I needed.

Soon afterward I had a mail inquiry for a spreader, I made the sale, had the spreader shipped to the customer, set it up, and collected the retail price. The wholesale price I sent to the company, and I sent the retail profit to the boy agent in whose territory the sale had been made.

It must have been the first $20 the boy had ever seen, and it was certainly the wisest thing I ever did. I could have sent the retail price to the company, and most likely the boy would never have been the wiser. But the windfall set the boy on fire, and he became one of my best agents. In all our dealings I never met him, but the orders kept coming in, and I don't believe anyone else got a cent's worth out of his territory.

However, not all of my dealings with agents were so pleasant. There was the old fellow in Meriden with whom the company was anxious that I establish friendly relations. The minute I set eyes on him I knew that he was operating on a shoestring. When I asked him if he would take my wife and me to board, he was mine. We didn't stay there very long, but long enough to get on good terms; we did some business—but I was careful to keep collections up to the mark. One day when I found the house empty and a crowd of salesmen clamoring for their money, I wasn't greatly surprised.

After the tumult and the shouting had died, I did a little detective work. The man's wife had a piano that she prized very highly. Guessing that she would not part with it easily, I went to the freight depot, gave the freight handler a dollar, and asked if this man had shipped a piano to anyone. He gave me the clue at once; the piano had been shipped to a fictitious name in Indianapolis. I wrote to the agent at that address and told him that some of his creditors were looking for him with blood in their eyes but that if he had any outstanding accounts and would send me a list, I would collect them for him, take out what he owed the company, and forward the rest to him; he wouldn't have to worry about my giving his address away. He sent me the list by return mail, and within a few days I was able to collect enough money to pay our account and to have some left over for him.

Another trying account was an agent in Waterbury, an old hardware firm. They had done some good business with us, but since the owner of the firm and the head of the implement department had died and the son just out of business college had taken over, our business had slipped badly. The first time I was in that vicinity, I went in to find out what the chances were of getting some business. When I inquired for the manager I was taken up an elevator to the top floor, where I found him surrounded by filing cabinets, desks, and stenographers, as far removed from control of the business as if he were on the moon. He looked wise and told me to see the man in the implement department. This young whippersnapper said that if anyone wanted anything he would order it.

Discouraged with the whole outfit, I went across the street to a competitor. This manager, who was out in front of the store, asked at once what he could do for me. He was talking to two drummers, so I did not want to interrupt, but as he had asked me, I said, "I want just one minute of your time. We always have had a contract with the firm across the street, but I have come to the conclusion that I'd rather have you take one of our machines and try to hurt us than to fool any longer with that stuffed shirt across the way."

The manager looked at the two salesmen, laughed, and said, "Go out and talk to Mr. Plumb. See what he says." I suspected that they were discussing the same young fellow and that my comment had come at the right moment. To Mr. Plumb I proposed that we make a contract.

"You have a nice mower," I told him, "and so have we. We have the best-selling rake and spreader there is, and I want to sell you one mower and as many rakes as you want—and then I'd like you to come out with me and canvass this country, to see if we can't get some business."

He said that was a fair way to put it, and we made a contract and arranged a date to go out. When we started he told me about an International spreader that had given them trouble from the start. It had broken down so often that the owner had given up in disgust and wasn't using it. This was especially discouraging because this man Pierrepont was a kingpin and others followed his lead. This was just what I wanted. If I could displace this spreader with a Worcester Kemp, I would have a start. When we went to see the man, he was very positive that no spreader would do the work.

"I can't hire any Daniel Webster to drive one of these things," he said, only he called it by its first name.

"You know what the churches did to convert the heathen. They sent out missionaries—and I am going to send one to you. I am going to put one of our machines in here and let you use it until you are satisfied, and if you are, I will swap for your spreader," I proposed.

He asked how much I would allow him for it. When I made him an offer of $45, he said, "You have made me a trade."

All I had to do was to start our spreader and see that the man knew how to operate it. From then on we had the spreader trade by the tail with a downhill drag. We sold a carload in a few days, just as fast as we could tell our prospects that we had swapped for the Pierrepont spreader.

I asked Mr. Pierrepont to store the old machine until I could sell it, and he said he would. I saw him only once afterward. At the Danbury Fair, when I was talking to a man who had stopped at my exhibit and said he was looking for a spreader but liked the International best, I looked up and there was Mr. Pierrepont.

"When are you going to sell my spreader?" he asked. "It is in my way."

I told him he had arrived just in time, as I was going to tell this man about his machine.

"Why, you can't tell it from a new one," Mr. Pierrepont said to help the sale along. "The paint is all bright and it is perfect."

"If it is so good, what do you want to let it go for?" the man asked.

Mr. Pierrepont walked away without a word, and I never saw him again. He hadn't thought of the question that everyone would ask.

It was good news when a rival's spreader wouldn't work, but not so good when one of ours lay down on us. Then it was up to me to think of some way to remedy the trouble. One, I remember, we sold late in the fall on spring terms to a loudmouthed fellow who ran a stock farm and bred heavy draft horses. In the spring he took the spreader out in the mud and got it mired, then refused to pay for it on the ground that its draft was so hard that his horses couldn't haul it. The agent sent for me, afraid this man would ruin his business. I promised to see him through but urged him to wait until I had time to help him out.

In August I went over to see what I could do. On my first

trip through this section I had learned that near this stock farm lived a man who raised and sold Morgan horses. There was a small war on between the two men, so my scheme was to sell the condemned spreader to the man with the Morgans, figuring that the squawks of the stockman might prove to be a boomerang if the Morgans could handle the spreader. I unfolded my plan to the agent, and even now I can see the grin that spread over his face.

At that time of the year the ground was dry and hard, and the draft was light. We went to see the Morgan breeder, and we didn't have to say a direct word. His eyes lit up as he saw what a weapon the other fellow had put in his hands. He sent his team over to the stock farm with an order from me, picked up the spreader, brought it home, and tried it out. I suggested that he try a load uphill, and the little Morgan team spread out the manure without a particle of trouble. The breeder couldn't get in the house fast enough to make out a check. I always have wondered just how the first man got around his loud talk about the spreader's heavy draft.

These were the sales that came off; but there were others when everything looked right and then at the last minute something queered them. I try not to remember the failures, because thinking about the times he failed to make good doesn't help a man; better forget them and put his mind on the times he had more luck. Still, there is one failure that does stick out in my mind. Following up a lead that one of our customers had given me, I drove out north of Hartford to see a young farmer who was doing pretty well with a small dairy. He hadn't thought about getting a spreader and wasn't at all sure that he wanted one. After I had convinced him of its value he said he wasn't ready to put the money in it right away, not even on the best terms I could offer.

It took me most of the afternoon to convince him that it

would be economy to get the machine. After he was finally sold on that idea, he said he wasn't sure he didn't want an International, because he knew their rakes and mowers and had confidence in them. This was the toughest, most cautious young Yankee I ever met. It took me another two hours to make him see the advantages of the Worcester Kemp. I had to use every sales argument in the book and a few that sprang out of the inspiration of the moment, but at last I thought I had him sold. As he saw me unfolding the contract and unlimbering a fountain pen, he began to fight shy again.

"My brother is my partner," he said, "and while I'm almost positive we'll buy one, I think I ought to consult him first. If you'll come around tomorrow I think I can give you the order."

The next afternoon I chugged jauntily up the drive, believing all the work done and that nothing remained but to get his name on the line. The young man heard the car and came out to the gate.

"I'm sorry to have put you to all this trouble," he said. "You have certainly sold me on a spreader. I know we've got to have one, but my brother thinks that since the International people have been so good about getting us parts for our mowers and rakes, it is only fair to buy their spreader." He smiled broadly as he held out his hand. I put on a smile too, and kept it on while I backed around and started down the road; but all the time I was cursing myself for being such a good salesman that I made a sale for an International instead of a Worcester Kemp.

These were the tough jobs, the kind that gave a man creases above his nose, but there was always something interesting to see along the way. I enjoyed stopping in the villages, talking to people, finding out how they lived, and getting their different philosophies of business. One day I walked over to a little marbleworking plant near a farm on which I was setting up a spreader. The owner of the plant told me that he cut only four patterns of tombstones and by limiting his designs he was able to cut a carload a week, which he shipped to Sears, Roebuck. He sent the bill of lading and got a check by return mail. Living in a remote section, he could hire his workmen cheaply; he had steady work the year round, and he was satisfied. That was one way of doing business; it was a good life, and he had no desire to expand.

Then, too, there were the visits with the agents who skinned their own skunks, as we say in Maine, and didn't need any help. These were fun—no problems, just visits to keep our relations friendly. One such agency was a firm of an old-timer and his son-in-law, who made such a good team that they were hard to beat. The old man had been a traveling salesman for a firm that made casket hardware. As he had dealt with undertakers, he dressed in a very formal style and looked as if he were about to conduct a revival meeting. He was known among the implement men as "Foxy Grandpa," because he was the very image of the comic-strip character. The son-in-law, on the other hand, was rough and ready. A dollar had to roost high and keep one eye open to escape them.

Whenever I could, I dropped off the train to see them, just for the fun of watching them operate. The last time I saw them they had taken out a license to mix fertilizer and were at work with a couple of mauls breaking up a pile of chemicals on the warehouse floor. From what they told me, I could see that they were not going to lose money on the operation. You would have laughed to see Foxy Grandpa in his ministerial suit swearing fervidly because the chemicals were so hard to reduce to powder.

EAST OF THE RIVER

THE territory east of the Connecticut River, south of the railroad that runs through Willimantic, was, I discovered, the most backward in New England. There were more oxen in this section than in all the rest of New England put together; you could see as many as a hundred yoke of them exhibited at Haddam Fair. If you looked out the window of your train when it stopped at a small station between the river and New London, you would often see a yoke of steers attached to a top buggy. The driver would pick up his visitor from the train, climb into the seat, flourish his long-lashed whip, and urge the steers into a gawky trot that would take them out of sight in no time, leaving a cloud of dust hanging in the air.

This was practically the last place in New England in which there were many oxen left, but then, everything about this country east of the river was a hundred years behind the times. However, traveling behind these oxen wasn't so slow as you might expect, for they were Devon cattle, dark-red, tall, high-headed, well-favored beasts that had long legs and walked at a very fast gait.

In the old days the farmers maintained that there was a lot to be said in favor of oxen; they could be used for harrowing and light plowing and were especially good for bringing in the hay, for they could turn their two-wheeled carts on a ten-cent piece and give you a nickel change. As

161

compared with a horse, they were inexpensive to keep and operate. All they needed in the way of harness was a yoke that any country handy man would turn out for $1.50, and they ate only half as much as a horse. Most farmers didn't feed them any grain at all unless they were being fattened for the market.

Then, too, every year a horse depreciates, while the oxen are making beef. Each year the farmer broke in a pair of young steers and sold a pair of heavy old oxen. It was easy money in his pocket.

All this I could understand, for in my father's day we had plenty of oxen in Maine. But the helplessness of these people in the face of a little work was beyond me, as it would be to anyone who had spent his boyhood doing the chores on a farm down East.

One night when I was waiting for a train in this section I saw a man with a Maine log rule in his hand, a scaler's bag for carrying records slung over his shoulder, and a woebegone look on his face.

"I guess you are from Maine by that log rule," I said by way of being friendly.

He jumped as if I had jabbed him with a pin and grabbed me by the hand.

"Are you from Maine?"

When I allowed that I was, he continued, "If I ain't glad to see somebody from God's country! I have been up here two weeks taking in telephone poles and dealing with these damned fools, and if I hadn't met you I guess I'd sure have gone crazy. Today in a camp where we are getting some poles a fellow asked me if it was true that they pay men in the woods in Maine $20 a week. When I told him it was, he said, 'I'm going down there to work next fall.' I said, 'They wouldn't let you carry the men's dinners in Maine.'"

The fellow was right. The men I met in this country did seem to lack the attitude toward hard work that we had been brought up on. For instance, there was our Niantic agent; at least he had sold a little stuff for us and was marked by the office as having a few prospects for spreaders. I dropped off the train one winter day and found him at work shoveling out the sawdust in his icehouse and getting ready to put up his year's stock of ice. At my suggestion he kept on with his job. I told him I would like to see some of the men at the ice pond, and he assured me that I could do just that, as all the men were hauling ice.

While we were talking, his hired man came in sight driving a yoke of oxen attached to a two-wheeled dumpcart with two cakes of ice on it, cakes that measured about eighteen inches square and maybe fifteen inches thick. If I had been loading such a team I would have put on ten cakes, and most men would have put on twenty.

The driver's face wore the most discouraged look I had ever seen.

"You can't do nothin' with this ice," he complained. "It's too thick, and so heavy you can't handle it."

I stared at him in amazement. All my life I had been used to handling ice in cakes four times that size and nearly twice as thick. As they stood there dumfounded by the impossible task, I went to the back of the cart, threw off the binding chain, tipped the cake up so that it rested on one edge and so reduced the friction on the bottom, pulled it to me, took it up, and threw it into the icehouse. Then I came back for the other one and threw it on the first without saying a word. Any sixteen-year-old Maine boy could have done it without a moment's hesitation.

When the man had recovered his astonishment he said to the hired man, "You'd better go back and get some more.

I guess we can handle it." With another long look at me, the hired man swung his whip and was off. I showed the man the trick of tipping up the cake so that it would ride on its edge and move easily, then followed the team down to the pond.

All the men in the neighborhood were there and engaged in the business of loading the teams with two or three cakes of ice. One old fellow had two yoke of oxen hitched to a four-wheeled wagon that might have belonged to Roger Williams. The rims of the wheels had been two inches wide in their youth, but now they were worn down to the quick and were full of weather cracks so that I was afraid the wagon would fall to pieces at my feet. The cart had to be set on a little ridge, and as soon as it was placed on the ridge it would slip down one side or the other. The whole thing didn't weigh 500 pounds, but the old farmer was stumped.

Grabbing the hind end, I called out, "Back up your team and I will look after this end." He backed into place, and it was like handling a baby carriage.

I left all hands staring and went on to the house of a farmer who was thinking of getting a spreader. The farmer and the hired man were at the icehouse, in front of which a team of big horses was backed. They had a set of blocks hooked onto a cake of ice and were pulling it up a slight incline with loud shouts of "Now! Now! Now!" As they pulled in unison on the falls, I climbed into the wagon, slid the other cakes up the incline and into the icehouse, and had them landed before these men got the first one placed. With no comment, I took up the matter of a sale, but they didn't have their minds on spreaders; they stood and looked at me in amazement.

When I got back to the agent's house for dinner he said, "You always will be known as the strongest man who ever came to these parts. You picked up those cakes of ice that they thought were too heavy to handle, you lifted the hind end of a wagon and carried it around, and you took the cakes of ice that two men were hoisting in with a set of blocks and falls and nearly buried them."

It would have been a pity to disturb this idea of me as a phenomenal strong man, so I didn't say a word. The only thing the matter with them was that they hadn't had a Maine upbringing. We were taught to do the job that had to be done with what we had to work with.

Although the people east of the river were short on muscle and good common sense, they were well enough off and lived very pleasantly in their pretty little white towns on the river or with a wide view of the hills. They didn't seem to need to work very hard for a living, so they were content with old-fashioned tools and ways.

One day when I drove up to call on a prospect—I was in the Maxwell on this trip—the woman who came to the door of the beautiful old farmhouse said her husband was down at the mill; if I wanted to see him I could follow the road through the woods. Leaving the Maxwell, I set out on the cart path through a good piece of timber, almost untouched, and finally came to a little river with a sawmill on the near bank, a weathered old building with hand-hewn chestnut timbers and a handmade water wheel, the kind that must have been used in my grandfather's day. The saw, which was making a faint buzz like an anemic mosquito, was the old up-and-down kind.

Inside, the farmer was cutting a few boards. He wasn't working very hard, and seemed perfectly willing to stop and talk. After we had discussed spreaders for a little while he decided he'd like to have one, so we started back to the house, swinging around to pass through an orchard in which the man had been doing some grafting. As he had no grafting wax, he had been using cow manure and clay, a method that my father had used successfully to produce Tom Gould's sweet apples, which were famous in our neighborhood, especially among us boys.

At the house we went through the parlor, full of fine old furniture, to the man's office at the side of the house. He sat down at his desk with its pigeonholes in perfect order and took out an account book. While he was looking at it a little fair-haired boy came in, smiled at me, and presently came over to stand by me. Putting his hand on my knee he asked me, "Do you know my mama?"

"No, I'm sorry, I don't," I answered.

"Well," he said, "she's awful nice."

The farmer looked up and smiled.

"That's a recommendation for you." He opened his cashbox, took out the full amount of the spreader, and handed it to me.

After I had started the Maxwell I waved good-by to the little boy with the yellow hair, who had followed me to the gate and who stood looking solemnly at the car. It puzzled me that these people should be so comfortably off and yet so content to live in the past.

On the way back to the village the Maxwell broke down again. This time I couldn't find a blacksmith who knew enough about cars to fix it, so a farmer hitched a pair of oxen to it and hauled it to the river for me. When a boat came along I put the Maxwell aboard and shipped it to Hartford.

Soon I worked up a good business in this territory. My agent in East Hampton, a rural community around a church-bell foundry, was such a good story-teller that I always enjoyed visiting with him. As chairman of the board of selectmen, he had many a rousing battle with the forces of evil, even sometimes with the better element. His third selectman was a rising young man who was highly thought of by all the old maids and widows because he sang in the choir and had such beautiful black whiskers. He was also a deacon and as good as gold, although he didn't have enough sense to come in when it rained.

In the town was a lady of easy virtue whose resort was frequented by the light-minded—and, it was rumored, by some of the men who ought to have been ashamed of such conduct. The good sisters of the church held a meeting and demanded that she be driven out of town. They presented their demands to the deacon, who came to the chairman of the selectmen to confer about the best way to do the job. The old man pointed out to the younger one that there was no evidence against the woman and it would be unwise to move against her on suspicion. There was no legal way in which they could enforce their demands if she resisted, but the deacon was determined to carry out his assignment from the ladies of the church.

Finally the old man said, "I'll go with you and sort o' back you up, but you will have to do the talking."

The deacon agreed to this; in fact, it seemed to be the very thing he wanted, so they got into the deacon's buggy and drove over to see the woman. The deacon in his best manner told her that she was a blot on the fair name of the town. The citizens did not propose to allow her to corrupt the morals of the young people, and they would give her two days to move out of town.

The woman came right back at him:

"Why, you old black-whiskered goat! You are just afraid that I will tell what I saw you and that old maid doing over back of Johnson's hill in the bushes last Wednesday night when I was after the cows. You just want to scare me and, damn you, you can't do it. I'm going to tell everyone I see about it."

By this time the deacon had found his voice and in a whisper he said to the older man, "Drive on." As the chairman started his buggy the deacon whispered, "What shall we do?" He was so frightened that all the fight had evaporated out of him. "I am ruined," he muttered. "She met us on the road when we were coming home from town and she made this all up."

"You can tell some folks that, and maybe they will believe it," commented the chairman.

"That's just the trouble," the deacon groaned. "Some won't. If she ever tells that story I am ruined."

"Well, you got into this scrape against my advice, and now I'll have to see what I can do about getting you out," the chairman promised, "but I don't want any help."

When he had rid himself of the deacon, he drove back and congratulated the woman on the success of her strategy. After they had had a good laugh about it, he said to her, "A woman of your talents is wasting her time in this place."

"I know it. I have a place in Hartford all picked out, and if that black-whiskered old goat will move me, I'll go tomorrow," she promised.

But the deacon refused to have any further traffic with the forces of iniquity; he hired a man to move her.

REPAIRS

TO BE able to set up our machines and repair them was almost as important a part of the business as to make the original sales. Nothing discourages an agent so quickly as to spend a lot of time wrestling with the parts of a machine he doesn't understand or to find himself selling a line that the company doesn't stand back of with prompt repairs when a customer's machine breaks down or isn't acting right.

So just before the haying season opened, the company would call me in to sweeten me up a little before they sent me out to find the bolts careless farmers had dropped in crankcases and to dig old splinters out of pine stumps that had got stuck in the knives of mowers. I liked E. P. Curtis. He was a wise and human old fellow who had seen a lot of history and had a knack of getting on with people; but his brother J. D., the treasurer, I couldn't make out. His attitude seemed to me that of a man who preferred to save a nickel by doing nothing rather than to spend ten cents to make a dollar.

On these occasions J. D. put himself out to entertain me. His favorite story was the one about the old Quaker shipowner of Philadelphia who was doing very well for himself by being economical with the truth. Once when he hadn't heard from one of his vessels for a long time and feared she had met with disaster, he went to his broker and asked what it would cost to insure her, without, of course, mentioning his suspicion that she might be lost.

The broker said he would let the Quaker know in a few days, giving himself time to make inquiries about the vessel. While he was waiting to hear from the broker the ship-owner learned that his vessel had gone down in a typhoon off the China coast with all hands aboard, so he wrote a note to the broker saying, "Friend John, if thee has not insured my vessel, please do not do so as I have news of her."

Guessing that his client had learned that his ship was safe in port and wanted to save the insurance, the broker wrote the Quaker, saying, "I have already insured your boat, and I'll send the papers right over." J. D. always told me this story when he took me to lunch, and chuckled with admiration of the canny Quaker.

After having listened to all the stories in his repertoire, I would start out grouchily enough to do repairs, knowing that there would be very little spreader business until the haying season was over. A lot of this work was unnecessary, or would have been if our machinery had been made more accurately. I had written the factory a number of times that they should have a template made so that the holes for the bolts in the shafts and the crossbar would come in line, but they were optimists (an optimist being a person who doesn't give a damn what happens so long as it doesn't happen to him), so they paid no attention to me. Consequently a lot of agents who were perfectly capable of setting up their own machines didn't want to spend their time fooling with them.

I was always figuring out ways of handling the work when I had to do it with no one to help, and had made quite a reputation for the speed with which I could set up a spreader singlehanded. Mr. Weldon of Simsbury advertised me by spreading the news that I could do it in an hour. He was one of our ablest Connecticut dealers; he ran a hardware store and a greenhouse and handled his business without bothering me unnecessarily, but he wouldn't tackle a spreader. When one that he had ordered came in, he would call up my wife and find that I was on the road and wouldn't be in until Saturday. By the time I arrived, he and my wife were frantic.

Usually I got in at noon. There was a train for Simsbury at about one o'clock, and I could catch one back in an hour and ten minutes. If I missed that one I had to stay over the week end.

Mr. Weldon would meet me at the train saying, "It's no use. You can't do it. There isn't time." To which I would respond, "I can do it all right if you will let me have a man."

The man would always be down at the freight car waiting. I would go down, cut loose the parts, throw them out on the floor where we would want them, and start him to setting up the front wheels while I worked the body out the door. As soon as he got the front wheels ready I would enter the kingbolt and push it out so that it hung by a hair on the platform. Then I put through the axle, hung the beater, put in the apron, and put on the wheels.

"Now all you have to do," I would say to the hired man, "is to turn the beater bars and put on the neckyoke and whiffletrees and the seat and footboard and the guards and so on."

"Yes, I can do that all right," he would say. So I would leave him to do more than half the work, and run to catch my train. That is one way to make a reputation. Another is to pitch in and help when you see somebody doing a thing in the wrong way. Any sensible man would have known better, but I never could resist.

For instance, as I was driving into the town of Newport one day, I passed a blacksmith shop in which a man was holding an iron rod against the crankshaft of a mower while another was striking it with a ten-pound sledge as if his life depended on his efforts. After watching them for a minute I said, "I once knew a man who made a good living by minding his own business, but my business is repairing mowers—and I might as well tell you that you can't get that shaft out by what you are doing. That is a McCormick mower, and the shaft screws on with a left-hand thread. I can tell you how to get that shaft out, and it will cost you sixty cents."

The man with the hammer growled, "How?"

"Take your big cold chisel, put it down in the pinion, hit it about half as hard as you did when I came in sight, and you will split the pinion. It will fall off, and then you can buy a new pinion for sixty cents."

He hit it, and it did. Then he looked at the mower and said, "Where in hell was you yesterday?"

The fact is, I never could keep my hands off of machinery, and I had to see things done right. Perhaps this was an inheritance from our village carpenter, who taught me to swear and throw a chalk line and gave me an unholy respect for good workmanship.

Old Joseph was the building end of J. and J. Philbrook. His brother Jeremiah, who got the firm's contracts to build churches, was a shining light in the cast-iron Baptist Church, but Joseph was a jovial soul who kept things moving on the job. He built Father's barn, which was the last one in town to be constructed of hewn timbers.

I remember how Joseph squinted and measured when he came to look over the timbers.

"I can't frame her by square rule," he announced. "I'll have to frame her by scribe rule."

Many people have tried to tell me what scribe rule is, but they have only darkened the mystery. I do know, however, that it has to do with the variation in size of hand-hewn timber.

The broadax man had already come to work on the logs that Father had hauled from the wood lot and rolled onto the skids. He would pull out a log, squint along it with disgust, roll it over, squint again, spit out about a pint of tobacco juice, and say, "How in hell do you expect me to get an 8 by 8 out of that! Look at that sweep, look at them knots!" But after a few more squints he would roll the log up, dog it, and say, "P'raps I can throw the line."

I used to watch him stick his dividers in one end, hang his chalk line on it, take a piece of blue chalk out of his apron pocket, and walk backward, chalking the line. Then he stuck a bradawl in the other end, fastened the line to it, and instructed me to hold my thumb on the line at a certain point where he would push the line out of its straight course to accommodate the sweep in the log. Snap would go the line, leaving a blue mark from one end to the other. Then he would give a few blows with his ax to test it and say that it would have to be ground. I was unanimously elected to turn the grindstone. It was difficult. I was fascinated to watch the timber take shape, to see the broadax flash up and down, to listen for the shearing crunch and watch the long hewing fall off and a square timber appear from the log; yet at the same time I had to estimate how soon the ax would need to be ground, so I could get away in time.

At night the broadax man would say as he departed, "There's an awful sweep to her, but if you'll turn her over and pile some timbers on her, she may straighten out." And she always did.

Then Joseph came with his men. He demanded and received big pay, $2.50 a day in comparison with ordinary saw-and-hammer men whom Father paid fifty cents and dinner for an eleven-hour day. But Joseph was worth it. Besides, he brought his son, who worked for his board and the opportunity to see a barn framed. The first morning, he got out his square and pencil and drew a plan of the barn on a piece of board, showing every timber in detail; then he put it behind the door and never looked at it again.

Joseph lisped and, like all the Philbrooks, he had enormous feet. Once his brother Jeremiah was holding revival meetings in the schoolhouse, praying and making great headway. Then the door opened, and Joseph came in and started down the aisle, catching his feet on the seats and making an awful clatter. Jeremiah stopped in the middle of his prayer.

"Will someone take Joseph by the head and turn him around and back him in?" he requested.

Joseph was the one who picked the apprentices for the firm. One of his men used to give an imitation of him interviewing a boy who wanted to become a carpenter.

"Now, young man, I'm going to ask you thome questions and I want you to answer right up prompt. Do you play cards?"

"No, sir."

"Thwear?"

"No, sir."

"Thmoke?"

"No, sir."

"Chaw tobacker?"

"No, sir."

"Drink rum?"

"No, sir."

"Go to dances and thtay out all night with thome girl so you ain't no good next day?"

"No, sir."

"Hell, you wouldn't ever learn thith business."

But when Joseph did turn out a boy after three years of

apprenticeship, there wasn't anything further he could learn about the carpenter's trade.

Because of Joseph, I never got over my liking for doing things with my hands, so I enjoyed repairing our machines even though somehow I got the dirtiest jobs on the hottest days of the year.

On one Fourth of July, a day so hot that it almost took the skin off of your hands to touch the sides of the buggy, I was driving through a back road in Vermont to fix a few old mowers. As it was a grubby job at best and the farmers were likely to be grouchy about the way they performed, I wasn't too anxious to get to the first stop; so I didn't overwork the horse. Dawdling along, I came upon a clearing with the little old house in it literally hidden from view by a crowd of boys. They were all sizes; the biggest one might have been twelve years old.

When I stopped, the boys gathered around. To my question about fireworks for the Fourth, they said they had none. It was my duty, I told them, to celebrate the Fourth, as it was a great day in our history, but as I was away from home I couldn't do it very well. Would they shoot off the firecrackers for me if I bought them? The boys assured me earnestly that they would, so I gave them $2 and left them in a daze.

That evening, when I was loafing in the country store at the next town, the two oldest boys came in with their father. The father bought first four packs of firecrackers and a small flag, and then he bought enough staple groceries to come to $2. They gathered up their bundles and left without noticing me, and it seemed to me that my money had been spent wisely.

I remember another fearfully hot July day, this one in Meriden. As I was setting up a spreader in the freight yard on the sunny side of the depot and was almost reduced to a grease spot, the company caught me with a telegram telling me to go at once to Colebrook, N. H., to help an agent at that point. I went, and arrived there on a Saturday night. On the next day, which was the Fourth, I sat in the hotel and watched it snow on the mountain across the river. It was so cold that the hotel started the fire and had steam in the radiators, or I think I would have frozen.

Our Colebrook agent, a very religious old deacon, had bought quite a bunch of stuff that he couldn't set up, and the next day I began to wrestle with it, not very well pleased to have been compelled to travel across three states to set up a lot of other people's stuff. The deacon's daughter and son-in-law, a minister, with their two boys of about six and eight years, were visiting their parents and made quite an audience for me.

In the spreader that I tackled first the boltholes were nearly the whole size out of line, and as I had no tools to work with, I had to whittle the holes out with my knife. As I got this bad job together, one of the boys made an observation.

"You swear," he said.

"Do I?"

"Yes," he answered sorrowfully.

"Don't you swear?" I inquired.

"No."

"Doesn't your father or grandfather ever swear?"

"No."

"Perhaps they don't know how," I suggested, and he allowed that they didn't.

"You go and get your father and grandfather to come out here and listen," I said, "and if these tools hold out they can learn to swear for nothing." He jumped down from his perch and ran into the house with the glad news. I heard horrified gasps from the ladies. After that, I didn't have an audience.

NO TIME FOR MINNOWS

*W*HEN the company gave me another boost in salary and said I could have Connecticut for keeps, I suggested that we have an arrangement by which I would profit when I got more business. That seemed fair to them, so they said they would work something out. They did; they offered me the same salary that I had received before plus 5 per cent on all business over $20,000 a year that I brought in. Since the previous year's business was $11,000, I didn't feel that they were going to impoverish themselves, but I agreed, as there was some extra business in sight. The company also inserted a clause in the agreement to the effect that they reserved the right to use me in other territories if necessary.

I went to work in earnest, and the prospects looked good. Around the end of September the company called me in and said they wanted me to go into Vermont. They had lost the salesman on the east side of the state and wanted me to take over his territory and rustle up some business. I kicked, but finally I agreed to go for a month if they would give me a man to train for the job. They didn't know of a man. Finally I dug up one who had some experience in selling and persuaded him to give the implement business a trial. He had been a sewing-machine agent, and I figured that after selling Singers to housewives, selling mowers would be easy.

The sewing-machine agents worked in teams of three, a doorbell ringer, an "agent," and a closer. The doorbell ringer was the prospector who scouted the territory, going from door to door and getting in on whatever excuse occurred to him, to find out whether or not the woman of the house had a machine, and if she had, whether it was an old one that she would be likely to turn in on a new one. The agent came along next, following up the doorbell ringer's list. His job was to get one of his machines into the house. He might tell the housewife that his wagon had broken down and ask her permission to leave his machine a day or two until he could return for it, inviting her to use it meanwhile; or any other tale that he thought she might believe. The third man, the closer, was a linguist who needed to speak at least half a dozen languages to close sales with the many nationalities that were represented in Connecticut.

My man Allen, who had been a closer, spoke a dozen languages, not too accurately but well enough to get a man's signature on a contract. To make a sale he told me he often settled for as little as a dollar a week. The crew got only $10 among them for a sale, and sometimes when business was bad they had to chip in and lend somebody a dollar to sign a contract. He was tired of the insecurity and wanted to get out of the business, and as he had some mechanical skill, he thought he might do better with farm implements.

So we started out. For a few days I kept Allen with me and let him hear me make a sale. Afterward I talked it over with him and impressed on him the most effective sales points. When he had become familiar with the implements we were selling, I listened to him do the talking. As he seemed to be catching on pretty well, I sent him out on his own while I went after several accounts that I wanted to handle myself.

As I was confident he would get along, I soon left Allen to his own devices. He turned out to be a good enough salesman, but he couldn't leave the cards alone. All of us played pitch for a few cents a point; a reckless player could lose as much as $2 in an evening, but very few salesmen whom I knew indulged in all-night poker playing. We were a hard-working lot and didn't hold with burning the candle at both ends. However, Allen couldn't resist poker and was soon staking on the game the collections that he had made for the firm. He didn't last very long after he had lost a couple of times.

By this time I had learned to concentrate on the big firms, so I went after the Howard Hardware Company in Bellows Falls, which was the leader in this line. When I inquired for the manager, a clerk said he was down in the storehouse setting up a spreader. That was the best break I could have hoped for, so I went down and found him cursing like a mad-man. The agent who had sold the spreader to him couldn't set it up, so he had to do it; and he didn't like it.

"I should think a man as smart as you are would handle a spreader that you could have delivered to you all set up," I commented.

He bit in a minute. "What do you mean?" he asked.

I explained that we could ship a car of seven all set up and ready to haul away. He objected that seven was a lot to buy, but I told him that if he would ride with me a day or two we could sell them and there would be no need for him to buy more than one or two for stock. He finally agreed to go out with me, and in two days we sold four or five. Eventually I persuaded him to come down to Worcester with me, and we tied him up on the entire line.

On the way back we talked about exhibiting at the fairs. As there were none in his vicinity, we discussed the idea of having a fair without grounds, showing the cattle in the va-cant lots and even in the streets, the fancywork in the churches and halls, the poultry show in a tent, and the apples in the vacant stores. It had worked out well in Connecticut, so I didn't see why it shouldn't here. The business people, I believed, could be persuaded to put up the money for really good prizes, as they would get it back out of the crowd, especially if no races and fakers were allowed.

The agent liked the idea. When he got home he went out and got $500 subscribed by the businessmen and had the best fair in the state. It drew 10,000 persons and was so good that the businessmen raised $1,500 for the next year, and the Pomological Society voted to have its next show in Bellows Falls.

On this trip to Maine I came upon a story that has always stuck in my mind as a typical example of the way a New Englander lets his conscience and his fear of what the neighbors will think torture him. Of course they aren't the same thing, but somehow New Englanders often mistake one for the other. Our agent in one village happened to be the sheriff. As we were driving out to see a prospect, we passed a big, lonely old house sitting back from the road in an open field.

"That's one of the queerest cases I ever had," the sheriff said, pointing to the old house with his whip.

He told me that a spinster, not too old but one of those whom the neighbors labeled as an old maid, lived in the house alone and had the reputation of being a bit queer. One morning early, as the sheriff passed the house with a load of produce for the market, he noticed a man leaving from the kitchen door. He shouted to the man, who ran to the river at the foot of the meadow behind the house, crossed on the steppingstones that were known to only a few of the neighbors, and disappeared in the woods.

The sheriff jumped out of his wagon, gave chase, and finally treed the man and brought him back to the house. He was a young Frenchman from the north woods, little more than a boy, and badly frightened. When the woman came to the door she screamed and charged that the boy had broken into the house and attacked her. It took the sheriff some time before he could quiet her and take the boy to the village jail.

Indignation ran high. The boy, who had no means, was defended by an inexperienced young lawyer appointed by the court. On the advice of counsel the boy pleaded guilty. He got off with two years in jail.

But the story which the boy told afterward and which these villagers who could put two and two together believed, was quite different. He was an itinerant worker helping with the haying on a neighboring farm. When it was nearly over they ran into a spell of bad weather and the farmer, rather than board the boy and two other workers, paid them off. They started to walk to town and on the way they bought some cider. The boy drank too much, so when they passed the woman's barn he decided to go in and lie down on the hay to sleep it off. The others went on.

The boy in the hay was awakened by someone climbing up the ladder to the loft. As her head and shoulders appeared above the floor, he saw that it was the woman from the house. Frightened, he lay still, not daring to move or say a word. The woman came over to the hay and stood looking down at the boy. Seeing that he need not fear her, he reached up, took her hand and pulled her down beside him. She did not want to get away and whispered "Shh" when a team passed on the road.

Later the woman invited the boy to the house and cooked him a nice supper. Before daylight she aroused him, went down to the river, and showed him the steppingstones and a path through the woods that led to the village. She invited him to come again, and told him to tap at her window and she would let him in.

According to the boy he had been visiting the woman for nearly two years, but when he was caught, she invented the rape charge in addition to that of burglary and deliberately sacrificed her lover.

The sheriff shook his head and said he never would understand women and the way they carried on over this thing they called love.

As it was fairtime, I took in the state fair at Lewiston; E. P. wanted me to supervise the display, and I thought this would be an opportunity to get rid of a few secondhand implements that I had taken in trade to make sales. One of them was a dimwit's dream of a spreader that the farmer was supposed to put on the chassis of his wagon after he had taken off the bed. The chief trouble with it—and it had a handful— was that it clamped rigidly onto the axles and gave them no play. Consequently, when the farmer tried to use it, he found that it was good enough in a straightaway but that he needed a whole county to turn it in; he couldn't do it in a four-acre field. An advertisement of this mechanical wonder in the *New England Farmer* brought in a good list of prospects, but most of them turned up at our booth and fell in love with the new Worcester Kemp that we were showing that year.

One of the farmers who hung around the booth for a couple of days was a husky young fellow with a particularly moonstruck look in his eyes. He would stare at the bright-red spreader like a cow looking at her calf, go away and gawk at the cattle, then come back and stare again.

After a while I got into conversation with him and learned that he was a mechanic who had gone to the country on account of his wife's health and was trying to make a go of it on the farm. He liked the land and was certain he was going to be happy on the farm, but it took more capital than he had to buy the equipment he needed. He was such a likable young fellow that I wanted to do something for him. Behind the tent I had a spreader that was in pretty good condition except for a broken ratchet.

"You are a mechanic," I told him. "If you can make a ratchet for this, I'll sell it to you for fifty dollars and two years to pay."

His eyes lit up like a pair of firecrackers.

"I'm sure I can fix it," he said. "And on those terms I'm sure I can pay for it."

He signed the contract and took his spreader home on a wagon. The next time I was in Maine I went to see him. He had paid the notes in full and had the spreader oiled and painted until it looked as though it had just been taken out of a freight car.

"It's acted wonderfully," he said. "I wouldn't take a hundred dollars for it." These are the moments that make a fellow feel that he's a pretty good sort after all.

Another prospect, who came around one evening just as we were closing up, leaned against the tent pole and asked about a spreader. His breath perfumed the air and his tongue was thick, but he seemed mighty pleased with himself.

"Had a good day," he commented to the world at large. "Had a good day. I've traded horses eleven times and now I have a better horse than I started with, $14 in cash, a grindstone, a setting hen, and a bushel of beans. How much do you want for that spreader?"

After making several good contracts, I went back to Connecticut feeling like a million dollars. It was almost the end of the year. On the first of January, when the company sent me figures for the business I had done during the year, they were less than my estimate, so I went down to the office to check up. I was dumfounded to find that they were not paying me a commission on the Vermont and Maine business, as it wasn't in my territory.

"Neither was I," I told them, "and it wasn't by my choice that I was off my territory. I had more business than I could do on my own grounds and went up there to help you out. Now I want my commissions."

They insisted that there wasn't any way they could do it, and I said I wouldn't stand for it, so there we were, deadlocked. I was mad all the way through, though I don't know why I should have been so surprised—their policy was in keeping with the treasurer's whole attitude about business. I had resented it in a lot of little things but never expected anything like this.

It didn't do me any good to reflect that I hadn't had as much sense as the old black crows that used to eat the kernels of my tender corn shoots in my garden on the farm. They were never fooled more than once. I kept thinking about the way I had tried to keep them out of my cornfield. First I had set traps between the rows, covering them with dirt and cultivating for several feet around them so all the soil would be disturbed, but these crows walked right around the traps and went on eating the corn. Then I had put up a blanket tent and stuck a broom handle out of it to look like a gun. For a few mornings the crows were cautious, but when they saw that it was only a scarecrow, they paid it no more attention. One morning I got up early at about dawn, went down into the garden, and crawled under the tent with a real gun. A few minutes after daylight there was a rustling of wings in the woods and the first crow flew down to reconnoiter. He cawed, "All right, fellows, come on," and the whole flock followed. I shot the first bird; the others wheeled and flapped back to the woods with the most indignant squawking you ever heard. They called a mass meeting, and for a little while the woods was full of angry cawing. Then they flew away in a black cloud and never came back. They felt that I had tricked them and they couldn't trust me any more.

Well, I had been tricked—and I wasn't going to stand for it. When I went home that night I wrote letters to two implement firms, saying that I wanted to make a new connection, and got a letter right back from each one offering me a job. The next week I notified the Richardson company that I was leaving them, and didn't that start the fireworks!

They insisted that I couldn't do this, and I maintained that I could, because when I went to work for them and the question of a contract came up, I had said I didn't want one. "Any time you don't want me, you say so, and I am done, and any time I am not satisfied I will quit," I had said, and they had agreed. Now I was not satisfied and I had quit. There didn't seem to be much they could do about it.

SKUNK SKINNING

THE firm whose offer I accepted was the Syracuse Plow Company, a substantial concern with a fine reputation. It made both steel and chilled-iron plows, specializing in the latter. In many parts of the country a steel plow is unsuitable because it won't scour; in other words, the soil sticks to it. Ordinary soil has enough grit in it to scour the steel plow, but in the sections where the soil is volcanic ash the chilled-iron plow is the only one that will cut cleanly.

The company owned the basic patent for these chilled-iron plows, which depended a great deal upon the skill of the workmen, because the iron had to be poured into the sand molds at exactly the right temperature. Another basic patent the company owned was one for the shifting hitch on the reversible sulky plow. Some sections used right-hand plows, others left. Ohio, for instance, was divided by a line north and south; on one side of the line the plows were all right-hand and on the other, left-hand. The company also made a road grader, a diagonal scraper with handles, which we sold to road commissioners.

As soon as I was called to Syracuse I was aware of a great difference in the caliber of the two firms. The Syracuse Plow Company lodged me at the best hotel and told me to hang around and get acquainted with the line and the factory.

It was a very interesting week; the foundry fascinated me, especially the department in which they poured the metal.

I liked to watch the moldboards being shaped and dropped all glowing into a tank of cooling liquid where they glowed under water for a time and came out so hard that they would almost cut glass.

In the shipping department I saw a trainload of plows marked for South Africa. They were a pitiful sight, the poorest sort I had ever seen. I was told that the Boer War had left the country so poor that this was all the South Africans could afford, but before the war they used to buy big gang plows that were drawn by sixteen oxen. This made a greater impression on me than an acre of history books.

One day the treasurer said to me, "Mr. Gould, you will find quite a lot of collections to make, some of them very difficult." I told him that I had had many such jobs, and it had been my policy to do something when I was trying to collect the debt instead of coming away with a hard-luck story and letting someone else finish it.

He looked at me a second and said, "Mr. Gould, that's just what I was going to say."

When I was out on the road I got a letter from him enclosing a protested check, a dishonored note, and an open account against a certain man. On looking him up I found that he had accounts in two banks. In one he kept his account good. The notes that he didn't mean to pay he made payable at the second. I finally got some money and farmers' notes and a note for the balance secured by a mortgage on a two-year-old colt and made payable at the good bank. This wasn't what I wanted, but it was all I could get, and I was in hopes it would wash out. The treasurer wrote that they hadn't expected to get such a good settlement and that he was very much pleased with what I had done. I was pleased, too, but it did cross my mind that in the past he must have had some dumbbells working for him.

When the company lost their Maine man who had represented them for years they had hired what the books call a "breezy Westerner" to take his place. Yankees call these fellows "windy." He had been down there a long time and wasn't getting anywhere, so the company divided the state into two territories and gave me the part west of the Kennebec River, a section that I knew well and liked. As the line was well and favorably known, I began to send in orders. In about a week I got a telegram to meet the sales manager at the West End Hotel in Portland. The first thing he did was to call me down because I had taken a room without a bath.

"You are not working for a cheap outfit. You are representing the Syracuse Plow Company, and we want you well taken care of," he insisted. When I recovered from the shock, he asked, "Tell me, how do you get around so fast?"

On a map I showed him how I worked up the Grand Trunk, then hired a team and drove twelve miles to a town on a narrow-gauge railroad to Bridgton. Otherwise I would have had to spend a day and ride 150 miles to make it by train.

He suggested that he go out with me a day or two; and this was just what I wanted. I took him to the toughest old bird in the state, a man whom I had tackled on my previous job, and slipped out, leaving him to carry the burden. He couldn't even make a dent on the fellow. When we came out he told me that he didn't want me to do that but to go right ahead as if he wasn't there. The next man I picked very carefully and got a nice order. When the sales manager left me that night he said I was doing very well and to keep up the good work.

Part of my luck was due to the man I followed. This Westerner didn't understand that the Maine farmers resented being slapped on the back and called "Bill," and he never tumbled to the fact that they were individualists who had special needs. It wasn't a question of selling them what you had but of selling them what they wanted. I had learned my lesson a long time ago when I spent a few months selling cider mills. One farmer who had held out against all the arguments of a flock of salesmen told me what was the trouble.

"Your mill," he said, "has a right-hand feed. Now my barn faces the other way; it is on a hillside so the mill can sit in only one spot, and a mill into which I can feed my apples directly from the barn loft must have a left-hand feed." I saw the man's point. After puzzling over the matter for a few minutes I figured out a way to shift the feed to the other side and made the sale in the time it took to write up the contract. The man had bought something that he wanted. I could have talked until the cows came home but I never could have sold him a mill with a right-hand feed.

This episode came to my mind when I went into Franklin County to sell a farmer on whom my predecessor had hammered in vain. The company wrote me that he had made three trips to see the man, and as this farmer was a kingpin in the neighborhood they wanted me to try again. I went, without much hope. The farm was a large, beautifully managed place for Maine; the owner seemed to be a real farmer. It was almost twilight when I arrived, so he invited me to stay to supper and spend the night. After I had told him what my business was I did not mention it again, for I had a feeling that it would do no good; the man wasn't going to buy.

That evening we had an unusually pleasant time discussing everything but plows. The next morning after breakfast, as I was preparing to leave, still without mentioning plows, the farmer walked out to the gate with me and said, "I'd have bought one of your plows years ago if they plowed even;

but I've seen them work. One blade cuts a deeper furrow than the other and makes the field look like a washboard."

"That," I told him, "was due to the carelessness of an assemblyman in our factory." The blades were adjusted by a simple mechanism on the side and could be pushed up or down to any position the farmer wished.

"If that's so, I'd like to have one," he said. "What else does the company sell?"

The company was pleased at my good luck, and everything was going along satisfactorily when suddenly the John Deere Plow Company, which was getting into its stride, bought out the Syracuse Plow Company, lock, stock, and barrel. They wanted the hitch, the chilled plow, and other things. There we were, all up in the air, none of us knowing how we stood.

While I was wondering what was the best thing to do, the Richardson Company came after me with a proposition to return as assistant sales manager at a marked increase in salary. I bit, and I am glad now that I did. If I had stayed on I should probably have died a traveling man and never have had my country store. And I would have missed a lot. A man doesn't get to be his own boss without learning some things that he never learns working for others.

When the sales manager outlined my new job, he said, "I don't know how it is, Gould, we never thought you were much of a salesman. You never ran up sales as spectacular as some of these crackerjacks we have on the road, but at the end of the year you always come out ahead."

I didn't see any use of saying so, but I thought I knew the answer. The other fellows spent their time making sales while I was trying to make salesmen, and in the long run it worked out better for me as well as our agents. It never made an agent feel very happy or cooperative to have one of the company's crack salesmen dash in and make a big sale over his head, maybe to his next-door neighbor, without letting him have a chance at the commissions. Maybe he wasn't on his toes and should have seen the chance himself, but such practices didn't make him any more eager to go out after business.

The new job should have been called "skunk skinning," for I was assigned all the dirty jobs that the traveling men couldn't do or didn't want to do. Some of them were practically impossible.

The company wanted me to live in Worcester, so I found quarters in the Argyle Hotel on Pleasant Street. When my wife and I entered the dining room for the first time, the head waitress came up with an affable manner and asked if there was any particular place we would like to sit.

"I am very fond of schoolteachers," I told her. "If there are any here, I should like to sit at their table." She said there was one, and I could sit at her table as well as not. She led us over to the table, at which sat the most unattractive old woman I have ever seen. I turned and gave the waitress a reproachful look. She snorted, put her hand over her mouth, and dashed out into the kitchen where I could hear her laughing for five minutes.

My wife did her best to repair the damage, and after we got acquainted we found our companion very agreeable. She owned a large block of stock in a fleet of ships that sailed to the West Indies and South America, so every summer she made the round trip to some Southern port without expense.

This hotel was a dangerous place for a single man. It was infested with old maids and widows who were skillful in stalking their prey. Every time a new man came to the house someone would come to my wife and say, "Mrs. Gould, did you see the new man? I think he is wonderful! Why don't you have a card party and invite him up? I'll get the refreshments." Then we would throw a card party, the new man wouldn't bite, and we would hear the comments of the disappointed.

One old widow who was infatuated with married life, or at least gave me that impression, said that she was going to spend all but a thousand dollars of her capital in search of a husband; then if she had no luck she was going to work. She was in raptures for a day or so when a young dentist came to the house and seemed to be drawn to her, but he only wanted to borrow from her. I thought she would have done better to save her money.

One of my first trips as assistant sales manager was to Vermont, to train a new man who was in charge of our exhibit at the Brattleboro Fair. The sales manager told me to be sure and see a man in Wilmington on the same trip.

To reach Wilmington, I found, would take two days, as I would have to take a train to Northampton, Mass., connect with a train to Hoosac Tunnel, and there get a train to Wilmington. After staying there all night I would have to take the same length of time to get back to Brattleboro; all this to get to a town that was only about twenty miles away across the mountains. My man at the fair was green and needed a lot of supervision, and I didn't want to be away for two days, so I hired an auto to carry me over and back in about three hours. I wasn't away from the fair for any valuable time and the cost was $10, very little more than my carfare would have been, so I thought I had made a good trade for the company. But I got a letter sternly admonishing me never to do such a thing again. Of course I did, as every traveling man will, although never unless they drove me to it.

Almost all of us have to put up with such irritations from the home office, but when we are on the road we feel that we are among friends and we enjoy our contacts with our agents, many of whom become our friends in that intimate and casual way in which two people are drawn together who may not see each other again for a long, long time. We can afford to be natural and kind and impulsive, because we don't have to think of all the ramifications such a friendship will have in our everyday lives.

One of these friends whose memory I still value was Mr. Hanson, of Hanson and Pingree, in Newport, Maine. When I was sent into Penobscot County for the first time, these two young partners struck me as the right sort, and I suggested that they stock our full line. This included horse cultivators, which were new at that time. Mr. Hanson was a little dubious about stocking such an unheard-of implement but he got out his new Ford, which had cost the enormous sum of $365, and we started out to see if we could sell a few. I did not realize at the time how well he stood with the farmers, but that afternoon we sold a mower and five riding cultivators. It was the best afternoon I ever spent. From that day the firm became one of our best agents. Now it is one of the leading hardware firms of the state. Mr. Pingree is dead, but Arthur Hanson is still active, a little older but looking about the same as he did that afternoon when I rode out in his partner's new Ford car. If all agents were like Hanson and Pingree, traveling men would have an easy life.

Another agent whom I remember with pleasure is a hardware man of Monticello, Maine. The sign over the door of the attractive store on Main Street read "Burrel S. Foster." I went in and met a gracious man who listened to me courteously. When I had told my story, he said, "I am sorry, but I have to buy in carload lots in order to get a freight rate that will allow me a profit. I have to have binders and so I must fill the car with all kinds of haying tools, potato planters and diggers, and cultivating tools, and I haven't room for your line."

I saw the force of his argument and told him that I hoped I could get a car near by in which I could put some of our specialties that he could use profitably. When I was about to leave, he asked if I would keep store for a few minutes; he wanted to step up the street. When he returned he invited me to sit down. "You can't get away until afternoon, and I'd like you to have dinner with me."

I said I wouldn't think of going in unexpectedly and causing a woman a lot of work, but he assured me that his wife was expecting me. He had told her while I kept the store. The kindness of total strangers, their willingness to be friendly and make our work a pleasure instead of a daily battle, was one of the chief attractions of the road.

Then, too, we were always meeting adventures that kept our minds from our troubles. Nobody could take himself too seriously when he tried to sell mowers to such fantastic prospects as the man in Wellington who had invented a new kind of windmill. Our agent told me about it as he drove me out to the man's farm, and there it was, standing on top of his woodshed, the queerest contraption you could imagine.

Instead of turning vertically when the wind blew, it moved horizontally like a merry-go-round. The sails were immense doors that swung out to catch the wind. When they reached the point at which they were of no use, they swung in and were furled until they swung around to the point at which they caught the wind and were again unfurled.

The inventor could have bought a conventional windmill for a small part of what he had spent on this wonderful idea, but he loved it. He had the mill geared to a wood saw and his hopes soared high. In fact, he was so busy showing us how the thing worked that we couldn't get his mind on mowers.

One winter day several years later I drove a friend, another traveling man who was a great whopper artist, over to Wellington, but at that time the inventor was so disgusted with his creation that he wouldn't show it to us. Oh, it worked all right, he said, but that was the trouble; it kept right on working and he couldn't stop it. He had forgotten to invent a brake. One day during a lull in the wind he had climbed up into the windmill to apply some oil, and it started again while he was inside. He had a wild ride until a flaw of wind enabled him to get out. After that he never used his invention, and there it stood like a goblin monument atop his woodshed.

We were disappointed, but my friend took a picture of it and it looked very impressive in the snow. During a three-day blizzard the next winter, as I was sitting cozily before the fire, I opened the morning paper. On the front page under an A.P. by-line was a story about the horrible plight of this inventor, who was trapped in his windmill while his neighbors were holding prayer meetings on the hillside praying for the wind to stop. And under it was the picture of the windmill in the snow. It gave me chilblains to read the story.

For days the inventor's mailbox was clogged with letters from all parts of the continent asking how he was after his terrible experience. It was a long time before he forgave me for my innocent part in the hoax.

FIELD TRIALS

ANOTHER one of my jobs as skunk skinner was to manage field trials and see that rival salesmen didn't put over fast ones on us. As the new spreaders came into the market some of the agents for the other companies, especially the big Western ones, believed all that the salesmen for their machines told them and were eager to challenge us. By this time I knew the weak points of the other spreaders and usually came off fairly well.

One test that I was drawn into was in southern New York, where I had sold one of our spreaders to a big breeder of thoroughbred Holstein cattle. As it was the first one we had sold in this vicinity, I went down to set it up and start it. When I got there I found that the International man had talked our customer into letting him send in an International on trial. He had made some very loud talk about the advantages of his spreader as compared to ours. The man was one of the misguided local agents who believed all the salesman told him and didn't realize that his statements were like a political platform, made to get in on but not to stand on.

If he hadn't been so green, he wouldn't have stuck his neck out quite so far. As it was he had stated that his machine had a lighter draft than the Worcester Kemp and would beat ours to a frazzle, not knowing that the International had an immense beater that worked well in the light strawy manure of the West but had a very hard draft for New England.

I was under no obligation to enter a contest, as I had a signed order, but I said, "Go ahead."

The farmer, who thought it was going to be a good show, invited all his friends to see it, and there was quite a crowd gathered around. One of the hired men opened the door of a pen where he had run a dozen bull calves for six months, fed them on skimmed milk, and bedded them with rye straw about five feet long. As fast as the straw got wet he had put in more, so the pen was filled about six feet deep with manure bound together with the straw. It was the worst mess I ever had seen, but I never said a word. I gave the farmer a look, he winked at me, and I saw that he knew what he was doing.

The two big hired men climbed in, started at the back of the pen, and began to roll up the manure like a carpet; by the time they got to the door they had a roll as big as a barrel. It was lucky for them that they were higher than the spreader, because they never could have lifted it off the ground, but they rolled it on and went back for more. When they had the Worcester Kemp loaded, they backed up the International and proceeded to do the same thing. I cut down the feed on mine to the lowest point, then went ahead and spread out the load; but I didn't do a very good job. The agent watched me with a sneer and when I was done said, "Now I'll show you the difference between that and a real spreader."

He had a powerful team, so he started out with his spreader in high feed. As soon as the beater struck that mass, it flew apart, the pieces filled the air, and all he had was a mess of junk. But he wouldn't give up; he brought in spare parts and got the spreader going—only to have it blow up again.

Finally he acknowledged that he couldn't spread it with his machine. I set back the feed for him, and we managed to get him unloaded and sent him home with a story to tell the International salesman when he saw him the next time. But

I never knew how the salesman got around that field trial, which was seen by every farmer in the neighborhood. As a matter of fact, it was hard for him to get a hearing after that.

Down in New Canaan a farmer's wisecrack helped me to pull off a victory. The New Idea salesman put one of their spreaders in against the Worcester Kemp, so I went down to see the battle through. The New Idea had two beaters, one above the other. The top one ran very fast and was designed to break up the bunches of strawy manure that are common in the West. The farmer at whose place we were holding the trial had a basement under his stable in which he stored a great amount of green-grass manure, sticky as heavy paint. This was the Ideal salesman's first acquaintance with the product. The load sagged down in the spreader so far that the teeth of the top beater barely dragged in it, and it threw a shower of thin manure on the driver. When he came in, having finished the first load, he said to the proprietor, "Are you going to try this damned thing again?" The owner said he thought they might want to.

"Then, by God, you either drive it yourself or get me an umbrella," the driver protested. "This is the damnedest new idea I ever saw; one beater throws the manure on the farm and another throws it on the farmer." The crowd howled, and the New Idea salesman soon withdrew. Nothing could stand before a crack like that.

Although it is much pleasanter to think about the trials that come off in victories for the Worcester Kemp, they didn't all work out that way, not by a jugful. When I was working in the blueberry barrens of Washington County, I came upon a set of conditions that almost had me stymied. The local agent at Dennysville and I were traveling about the country when we found that at Lubec the sardine factories made, as a by-product, a large amount of fish waste that was in great demand as a top-dressing for grassland, but the gulls were finding it vastly easier to come inland and pick it up off the fields than to retrieve it from the ocean. This situation suggested a new phase of the spreader business, at least one that I had never heard of. I thought it over and decided that it was a question of reducing the fish waste to such small particles that the gulls couldn't pick it up, and as we had a special low feed, I thought the Worcester Kemp could do it. We arranged for a trial, and it was a great success. The farmers followed the machine exclaiming, "I'd like to see the goddam' gull that could pick that up."

When we had sold a number, the idea got about that the spreader could do anything. A road commissioner wanted one to spread gravel on certain roads to which he gave a light coat every fall, so I sold him one on trial but cautioned him that although small stones would go through well enough, he must be careful not to load rocks.

After watching several loads spread, we left to see other prospects. A few days later we got word that the machine was a failure. When we returned we found two of the beater bars with the teeth knocked out. On investigating we learned that some of the men, fearing that the spreader might lose them their jobs, had loaded on it a rock as large as two men could lift. I found the rock and showed it to the commissioner. Finally I arranged to send him some more bars, so the sale went through. This was the first case of sabotage that I had met.

Another of my jobs was to go out and help agents who were not doing very well. We had one Maine man in Franklin County who had been out three weeks and hadn't made a sale, so the sales manager sent me up to see what could be done.

As soon as I talked to the young fellow I saw that his

trouble was a lack of confidence; he had never done any big business, so when he called on one of our local agents who happened to be a storekeeper and heard the man sell molasses by the hogshead and tenpenny nails by the keg, his mouth fell open and he couldn't get up the nerve to make the sale. I knew how he felt, because when I first started out I had so little confidence in myself that I was afraid to tackle the big customer. It took me a long time to learn that it is just as easy to sell the big ones as the little ones, so it's best to lose no time fishing for minnows.

The first snow had fallen, so we hired a sleigh and set out for Temple. We drove up to the general store, which was a pretty big concern, as it served the whole countryside. I waited until I could see the manager, then took out a photograph of our rake and said I wanted to sell him a carload.

"Is that the New York Champion you have?" he asked.

"No," I told him, "it's the Worcester Champion. Its teeth are a thirty-second larger than those of the New York Champion and they don't break off so easily."

"Give me twenty-five," he said.

From that we went on to rollers. which I sold from photographs.

"I couldn't buy but two," the manager decided.

"Write that down, Mr. Jackson," I instructed our agent, and from the corner of my eye I could see his hand trembling.

After he had written up an order for nearly $900, we went out and climbed back into the sleigh. For about a mile we drove along in silence. Finally Jackson, who had been staring straight ahead of him, said without looking at me, "Why don't they talk that way to me?"

"You haven't been talking to the right fellows. There are some big dealers up here, and you might just as well go after them as the little ones."

This boy (he couldn't have been more than twenty-one or twenty-two) looked at me with such a puzzled, appealing face that he reminded me of all my own early quakings and misgivings. I saw that I'd have to build up his faith in himself. The first thing to do was to make him feel that we were fellow travelers, not a green salesman and an instructor.

It had stopped snowing, and the trees were covered with a fuzzy white coat, as they often are in the fall when the snow is wet. As we slid along I kept thinking of the way they looked when I was a boy and had the job of cutting wood. Jackson had done it, too, so we were soon reminiscing like a couple of old-timers. He told me how he used to get up at four-thirty of a January morning when his room was so cold that white frost stood on the walls. In the night, nails contracting in the intense cold would break off with a noise like the shot of a cannon.

I told him about our lantern that Father had made by punching holes in a sheet of tin, rolling it into a cylinder, putting a door in it and a socket for a candle. A few feeble rays struggled through the holes, enough to help me find the pitchfork and the ladder. I would pitch down the hay, feed the oxen, and give the rest of the cattle a little to quiet them, then put up a big bagful of hay for each yoke of oxen or steers and carry them out to the sled to be ready for starting for the wood lot after breakfast.

Father and I put up our dinner before breakfast—that was a rule for men working in the woods; otherwise they wouldn't have enough. In would go biscuits, slices of mutton frozen hard, doughnuts, cookies, hogshead cheese, a tea pail, tea, and sugar. We always took some apples, but these went into our pants pockets to keep the fruit from freezing.

After a light meal of fried potatoes, a slice of ham as big as my hand, about four eggs, three or four doughnuts, a piece of apple pie, and two cups of coffee, I would yoke the cattle and start for the woods, leaving Father to come later with the horse. Before I had gone half a mile, every hair on the oxen would be covered with white frost and I would be running behind, kicking my toes on the bunk to keep from freezing. My cowhide boots would be frozen as hard as iron. The oxen would hurry along, every hoof rattling, their horns clashing on the yoke, the chains jingling and the sled runners squawking and grinding over the dry, frozen snow. When I turned into our woods at about daylight, the temperature seemed to go up twenty degrees. The thick fir and spruce growth broke the wind, and by the time I reached our lot it wasn't too bad.

Jackson laughed and slapped the reins on the horse's back. "Tell me," he asked, "after you had started a fire were you sissy enough to hold your boots in the smoke to take out the frost? And at about eleven-thirty would you chop open a water hole, fill the tea pail, and pile wood on the fire, hang the pail on the tea stick, and set your frozen dinner pail to warm?"

We exchanged fantastic stories about the amount of food that men in the woods will eat. I wasn't taking liberties with the truth when I told him what I used to consume when I was sixteen years old and had my first job cutting wood for a man for sixty-five cents a cord. He boarded me for fifty cents a day, his own offer, but I feel to this day that I cheated him. Both of his sons had left home, and his wife liked to see a boy eat. She must have had a good time that winter. At first she put up my dinner in a pail that held about three pints. At night she asked, "Did you have enough dinner?" and when I answered "Yes," she said, "I don't believe it, and I am going to send some more." Soon she made the hired man hitch up and bring me a warm dinner.

One morning the old man said at breakfast that it was thirty degrees below. As I started on the mile or more to the woods, it was beginning to get light, and there was a pink tinge over everything. From every chimney streamed a column of smoke a mile long. I made a fireplace against a blowdown as soon as I got into the woods, and lighted a fire. The heat was reflected from the brush shelter, and I had a seat of cordwood and was pretty cozy. At about eleven I began to get hungry and to listen for the bells of the pung. The horse was one of the kind that takes a step once every twenty minutes, so I would hear a "bong," then a pause and a "dong"; he was coming slower than cold molasses. Finally he reached my fire, and the old man handed me a ten-quart pailful of dinner. In the center was the original pail of beef stew, full of potatoes and onions and dumplings. Around it were sandwiches with thick slices of cold roast pork for a filler, half a dozen doughnuts, and two pieces of apple pie, about a quart of gingersnaps, and three big Northern Spy apples. I finished all but the apples, which I put in my pocket in case I got hungry before night.

"And at the end of the day," said Jackson with a sort of faraway tone to his voice, "do you remember when you started for home with a full load on the sled, how the bridle chains on the hind runners sang as they checked your speed down the hills, and how the sun went down and a cold wind sprang up and a little loose snow would drive ahead of it, writhing over the hard snow, falling into the road, and holding you back like so much ashes, and how the tired oxen would walk slowly, and you would lay your face against the near ox to warm it, then turn around and walk backward to warm the other side? And when you reached the driveway, how you had to fight to keep the steers from turning in, but you finally got them to the piling ground, and when they were unhooked they made for the barn without a driver? Then after you unyoked them, tied them in the barn, and fed them, you could go into the house to supper."

"And after supper," I added, "you had only to unload the sled and get out the skillet that held the tallow and lamp-black (ours had one leg broken off) and grease all the boots in the family to make them waterproof for the next day. And last of all you heated a soapstone, wrapped it in an old blanket, and carried it upstairs to put on the pillow, then down in the bed for your feet. You removed your coat and vest and, if it wasn't too cold, your pants, and jumped into bed, and the next minute your father would shout, 'Time to feed the cattle.'"

Soon there was a brotherly warmth between us, as though we had grown up together. Jackson was feeling spry enough to tackle a nest of wildcats, so I suggested that he take the team and try his luck at Strong.

"I'm going to see Croswell Brothers at Farmington Falls," I told him. "Clyde Croswell is pretty high-tempered—he ran our last agent out of the store—but I got a few orders from him when I was selling Syracuse plows and we get along well enough. He does a big business and is worth trying, but I may get a licking and I don't want any witnesses."

So I drove to Farmington Falls and went to call on Croswell Brothers. The store was still called "Brothers," although the old man who had been one of the original brothers had sold out to his son several years earlier. After standing around a while I got a chance to speak to Clyde. When he heard what I was selling, he flushed a turkey red and shouted, "I don't want any. I don't want any."

"All right," I said; but I did not hurry out, for I figured he might cool off and change his mind. While Clyde was shouting to me, an old gentleman had come in from the warehouse. He came over, introduced himself as the elder Mr. Croswell, and asked me what I was selling. When I said the Richardson implements, he took me to the warehouse and showed me around. The sheds were full of buggy parts, wheels, axles, and bodies, because the company supplied most of the carriage dealers in the vicinity. The old gentleman inquired about Mr. Curtis, who had been a friend of his when old E. P. was on the road.

"I'll go in and talk to Clyde," he offered, but he didn't seem to do much good, because Clyde called out, "If I want anything, I'll order it."

That night I wrote to Mr. Curtis and asked him to write to Mr. Croswell and send an autographed photograph of himself. E. P. sent me the carbon of the letter, and it was a masterpiece, all about the old times and the pleasant memories he had of Croswell Brothers.

I put the Croswells down as one of my failures and thought no more about the matter until I met Jackson a few months later.

"My God," he said, "if you ever did a job you did it on Clyde Croswell. I can't tell you how many mowers and whatnot they have bought. The company wrote me to go up and help Croswell, so I did; and when I got there I found the yard chock-full of mowers. I supposed they wanted me to set them up, but Clyde Croswell said, 'Hell, no, I want you to sell 'em.' I took out his big new Buick and sold all over the country."

FAIRS

O_{NE} part of my new job that I liked especially was the fairs. To be sure, I had been attending them every year in my territory, setting up our exhibits and gathering in the prospects; but now I had a much wider radius, all of New England, and in the autumn I was kept on the go from one fair to another, supervising our men and our shows.

In Maine the implement season began with the Bangor Fair, held the last week in August. Usually I arrived a day early to superintend the setting up of our machines. The spreader caused no trouble, as it was left stored on the fairgrounds, so all we needed to do was to get it out of the shed. Other firms also stored theirs from year to year.

One day, when all the members of the fraternity were busy getting our shows ready, we were bothered by a representative of the International Harvester Company, who had been told that there would be a spreader of his in one of the sheds but couldn't find it. I thought it likely that some local agent had made a sale and taken the spreader and that the record of the sale hadn't gotten around to the representative, but he didn't think so. As he kept bellyaching about his spreader and the fair authorities, who didn't seem to take his loss seriously, one of the representatives said, "I wish someone would shut him up."

"I will," volunteered another. When the International Harvester man came around with his story, the other representative said, "It is ridiculous that the fair authorities don't get the man who stole your spreader. I can tell you just where to look for the thief."

"Where?" asked the International Harvester man.

"At the insane asylum. No one but an insane man would have taken your spreader when he could have got one of ours."

I never saw a man get so mad over an attempt to help him. The madder he got, the more the crowd laughed. Finally he shut up and took himself off.

One fall the fair authorities had so many side shows that they had to put Kiko the Wild Man next to us. It was said that Kiko worked in a livery stable in Bridgton during the rest of the year. In the fall he and some of his gang hired a tent and exhibited him dressed in bathing trunks and chained to a post with massive chains. As he was under-sized, repulsive looking, and covered with coarse black hair, he was, to put it conservatively, very striking.

Sometimes the ballyhoo distracted our prospects. One afternoon as I was talking spreader to an old farmer, the barker began to bang on a gong that drowned out all other sounds, and a moment later a man came out from the tent carrying on a two-tined pitchfork a cow's shinbone much the worse for age and wear.

"Hurry, hurry, hurry! We're going to feed him. We're going to feed him," the barker kept repeating the raucous cry.

The old farmer leaned forward and asked, "Is that the same fellow you had here last year?" The barker said it was.

"I thought so. Same piece of meat, too, ain't it?"

I never saw a showman's attempt to advertise his wares so put out of gear by a few words. If you could have seen that bone with the few shreds of meat dried on it, you would have appreciated the old farmer's comment.

Sometimes we were almost deafened with cries of "See Big Annie, she weighs 700 pounds!" "The largest horse in the world—weighs 3,700 pounds!" "The fattest ever seen! Nine feet around his middle!" "Kiko the snake eater—eats 'em alive!" These were too much for a French Canadian who was pretty well lit. He kept the crowd in an uproar with his cries of "See Little Annie. Nine feet around her waist. Weighs 3,700 pounds and eats 'em alive, eats 'em alive."

At the Lewiston Fair we were luckier in regard to the midway, but we had other difficulties; our space was always at the end of the dining rooms and near the grandstand. As the comfort stations were some distance away, the men began to go behind our spreaders to urinate, and it soon became a nuisance.

One of our men, who was something of an electrician, set about remedying the defect. He got a sheet of galvanized iron and some batteries and a buzz coil, and soon had his trap set: one sheet of iron to stand on, one against the spreader for a target, and a switch at a convenient point. We wet everything down, to make a good contact, and were ready. When a man came along and made for his favorite spot, one of us would close the switch. A minute later we would hear an agonized howl and see a man come out on a run and make for the comfort station. All the implement men were onto the game and we had a lot of laughs, but I'm afraid we lost some customers for our line.

Much like a Maine fair was the one at Great Barrington; it brought out a crowd of mountaineers who reminded me of the down-Easters. The only time I attended this fair I arrived a day late. Our man who had the territory was expected to set up the spreader and have it ready for me, but he had gone on a toot and hadn't touched it. Annoyed, I got to work and, as always, soon had a crowd of spectators.

When the job was well under way I had to raise a wheel and prop it up so that I could turn it and roll on the chain. We always took care of this when we unloaded a spreader, but this one was flat on the ground and had to be handled by the strong-arm method. Finding a whiffletree that was of the right height, I gave it to a boy and told him to slip it under the edge of the spreader when I lifted it from the ground. The crowd burst into a loud bellow of laughter.

There is a trick to lifting a heavy load, a way of bending the knees and making the big lift with the knee joint. I backed up to the wheel, grasped the spokes, and squatted until I had a good purchase, then threw my whole strength into it. The wheel came up, the boy put the whiffletree under it, and I went on with my work.

A tall old fellow who had laughed when I offered to lift it walked up to the wheel, put his chin on top, grasped the spokes, and tried it. Of course he couldn't start it. He called a friend, and they both took hold on opposite sides; but in that position they were much worse off, so the two together couldn't budge it.

Puzzled, the old fellow came to me and asked, "Mister, how much does that damned thing weigh?"

"Just as she sets there she weighs about a ton," I answered.

Amid the shouts of the crowd, he asked, "How much do you weigh?"

He got a big laugh. However, none of the crowd had stopped to consider that only a small part of the weight was on the one wheel, and, no doubt, they had never heard of taking advantage of a lift. As I said before, it is worth a lot to a man to be brought up in Maine, where you are expected to do what has to be done with what you have to do with.

After I had set up the spreader and sobered up the agent,

I wandered over to a tent in which a mountaineer was exhibiting a captured moose. His prices were ten cents for one or a quarter for the whole family. A man came along, laid down a quarter, and said, "I want my family to see your moose."

The old farmer looked out of the booth and asked, "How many are there in your family?"

"Eighteen," the stranger said.

The old farmer handed back the quarter.

"Here's your money. Go right in. It won't cost you a cent. It is worth as much for my moose to see your family as it is for your family to see my moose."

In Vermont the great fair was the one held at Middlebury. The crowds that visited it were very different from those in Maine. Middlebury is the center of the sheep-raising industry, and the Vermonters have money; they do things that would fill a Maine man's soul with horror.

One year there was a free-for-all race with a purse of $1,000 and a side bet of $10,000 between the owners. One owner was Farley, the strikebreaker from Plattsburg, N. Y., and the other, a Vermont farmer. Farley was a character. He kept on tap a gang of hard-boiled fellows who guaranteed to keep the cars running—they were mostly horse and electric cars in those days—and did it with pick handles. On a moving car a husky man with a pick handle could do a lot to induce a striker not to tip over the car. The race was for blood, and no holds barred. Farley's horse had many admirers, and a lot of money was wagered the night before the meeting. The lobby of the hotel was filled with partisans, and each side was sure that it would be a walkover for its horse.

On the day of the race the excitement ran so high that at about three o'clock some of the implement boys proposed that we shut up and go to see the race. It was obvious that we weren't going to do any business. I didn't take much interest in racing, but it wouldn't look well for one man to queer the game by sticking out, so we all closed our shows and went over to the track. I remember the howls of derision that went up from the boys when they noticed me reading *The Saturday Evening Post* while the big race was going on.

It was packed with thrills for the fans. Each horse won a heat. As they came into the homestretch on the last heat, the Vermont horse came up on the outside, and Farley, who was driving his own horse, swerved to shut off his rival. He was set back for it, and the heat and race were given to the Vermont horse. You can imagine the excitement. The arguments that went on that night would have settled the coal strike.

At that same fair a ballgame was played by a nine, all of whom were brothers, and their father was the umpire. They had come from a mountain town near by and were of all ages from sixteen to forty. The old man, who must have been sixty, looked as though he could do as good a day's work as ever. These boys were a hard-hitting bunch and won handily from a college nine.

In Connecticut the important fairs were the old Connecticut State Fair at Berlin, the Charter Oak at Hartford, and of course the Danbury Fair, the biggest of them all. We always showed at each of them and did a good business.

It was at the Berlin Fair that I got in wrong with my wife and learned by this bitter experience to keep my mouth shut. Near our show there was a concession giving away so-called "canaries." I heard that they were furnished by city slickers in New York who caught English sparrows in great quantities, dyed them with Diamond dyes, and sold them as young canaries. They had a streaked appearance, but so do young canaries.

Anyhow, the fakers were giving them as a prize with a ringtoss game. You paid ten cents for ten rings and threw them at a stand with a variety of objects on it, and you won anything over which you could throw a ring. I bought ten rings, threw them over, and won a canary.

A woman who was standing near me said, "Look at that. He got one the first time, and I have been trying all day and can't get one."

"Please take this," I offered. "I want it about as much as I do a wooden leg." She took it with profuse thanks, and I never saw her again.

The next day my wife came down, saw the canaries, and wanted one. Foolishly, I told her that I had won a bird the day before and had given it away. Then the fat was in the fire. I had to tell her to whom I gave it; and, at that, she never believed me. Then I had to try for another. I spent $2 and never got so much as a tailfeather.

For days after that I had to listen to my wife cry, "Why didn't you keep that canary for me?"

"What on earth do you want with one of those things?" I would protest, but she always came back with, "I wanted it."

"You haven't even got a cage," I would point out. (The birds were delivered in a cage made of wooden slats and hardly big enough to house a June bug.)

"I saw a nice one yesterday for five dollars," she would answer. It did me no good to blow up and rave about a woman who would go out pricing birdcages when she didn't have a bird. All she answered was, "I wanted it."

The fair at Charter Oak in Hartford was the big horse-racing event and a great fair for implements. One year when there were a lot of new spreaders on exhibition, we heard a lot of boasting about which had the lightest draft. I knew that ours was as light as any and lighter than most, but there was no such thing as a light-draft spreader, and I got more attention when I said so than if I had claimed more.

Some of the salesmen asked me if I would go into a field trial, thinking that I would refuse and they would be able to say that I was afraid. I said "Yes." We had a new spreader that year, too, so I phoned the factory and asked them to ship me a pair of shafts. On the Sunday before the fair opened, I took off the pole, put on the shafts, and spread out a load with one horse. I put the thing together again and was ready. If they wanted to claim easy draft, I would spread a load with one horse.

On Monday the contestants came and told me they had given up the idea. Someone had spilled the beans. But I had the shafts there and offered to bet that I could spread a load with one horse. It had a good effect, as we sold all the spreaders that were sold.

The Danbury Fair was the finest of them all. Today, I am told, it is little more than a mammoth carnival; but in those days it showed the finest horses, hogs, sheep, and cattle that you could see in the country, and the plowing and weight-hauling contest for oxen paid good money. The exhibits of the womenfolk also took off a lot of fancy prizes.

For Fair Week the company always took a front parlor with two beds in it at a small hotel and entertained the agents. The residents of Danbury always let rooms during the week and I suspect that some slept on the floor to rent all available space. Even so, it was next to impossible to get a room. Ours was a big barn of a place. At first I thought the price excessive, but not after things got under way.

One afternoon a man came to the booth and introduced himself as our agent from east of the river in a town that

I had never visited. I made him welcome and asked if he was staying overnight. He said that he was if he could find a room. I invited him to sleep with me, so he made our room his headquarters and at night went downtown with us to see the fun.

The Danbury people like to get the last dollar out of the crowd and had arranged a carnival for that purpose. Fakers and nigger dodgers were set up in alleys and on every spot where one could operate. The markets were loaded with ripe tomatoes, and half-bushel baskets of them were displayed everywhere for twenty-five cents. A student with half a jag on bought a basket and threw the tomatoes at a surprised Negro before anyone could stop him. From then on the fun was fast and furious. Some shows shut up, but the wise ones bought tomatoes, offered them at three shots for five cents, and cleaned up.

The Yale boys were armed with yardsticks given away by a stove company. One of them had two yardsticks. He put them together, and when he met a girl he waited until he had passed her, then gave her a smart blow on a prominent part of her anatomy. The first time it happened, the girl leaped a foot in the air, then turned around, ready to blast the guilty wretch off the face of the earth.

But everyone looked innocent, so she provided herself with two sticks and went forth for revenge. I was watching the fun and laughing, when I got a whack that made me jump. My assailant was an old lady in a sedate black straw bonnet, the kind you would pick for the ideal grandmother, and she was just as full of fun as the rest. The crack produced by the two sticks slapping together was as loud as a pistol shot. When the whole crowd was armed it sounded like the Fourth of July.

PLEASURES OF THE ROAD

IN SPITE of the irritations with the home office that are part of almost every traveling man's life, we enjoyed many pleasures of the road—the little inns where the cooks remembered what we liked, the friends we made at our favorite stopover points on Sundays, and the glimpses we got into the lives of the people we met. These glimpses were like a continual theater, sometimes a comedy, sometimes the tensest kind of drama. But we hardly ever saw the end of the play, just the scene or two in the middle, enough to whet our interest.

On one of my trips to Brattleboro I came upon a family that by all the rules of the game should have been headed straight for tragedy; but it was one of the happiest ones I had ever seen and just goes to show you that every once in a while old human nature has a good laugh at us.

One morning I stopped to call on our agent in a small Vermont town. As it was a pleasant day and I had plenty of time, I drove out into the country with him to help put over a sale. We stopped at a beautiful old homestead. Everything looked neat and prosperous, the barns were full of well-cared-for stock, and there seemed to be no reason why we shouldn't make a sale.

A young man came out to see us—as handsome a specimen of humanity as I have ever seen, six feet tall, as wide across the shoulders and slim as an ax handle, with brown, curling hair and a very pleasant expression but no unusual signs of intelligence. A little girl of about two years clung to his hand all the time he was talking to us, and finally she begged to be taken up. He picked her up, she put her arms around his neck, laid her head on his shoulder, and seemed to feel that she was just where she wanted to be.

After we had talked a while, the young man suggested that we go into the house, where we met his wife, who was at the ironing board. She had a very intelligent face and a commanding presence, and struck me as being about twice the age of the young man. She remained at the ironing board and continued her work, but she listened to our talk and occasionally threw in a word that went to the very bottom of the matter.

It seemed that these people needed a spreader at once but couldn't pay for it then, so I suggested that as the season was nearly over I ship it on spring terms to be due the first of May. The woman said at once, "We can do that very nicely," and we closed the deal.

As we drove back I asked the agent to tell me the story behind that couple. The woman, he said, was the only child of a well-to-do farmer who had sent her to the best schools and to college. She graduated with high honors, became a teacher, and in a short time was principal of an exclusive Southern finishing school for girls.

When the woman was in her late thirties, her father had a shock and became a helpless, bedridden invalid. The daughter came home, took care of her father, and ran the farm with the help of the hired man. Some time later they came to town one night and were married by the minister. This caused a lot of talk, but it wasn't a patch on what was said when it turned out that they had need of haste. The little girl came along in about four months.

I have never forgotten that woman and her husband, because it seemed to me that she was living in the midst of drama. For it was the woman's story; of that there could be very little doubt.

I like to think what a difficult decision she had to make. She had to abandon her life's work and the luxury in which she had lived, for the drudgery of the farm. As she watched her youth fade she turned in desperate loneliness to this natural, uncomplicated farmhand who had the attraction of a friendly and remarkably handsome animal. She might have avoided the result of her folly, but she chose the hard way. If you could have seen the little girl as she laid her head on her father's shoulder, you might have thought, as I did, that the mother counted the world well lost for love.

In addition to the pleasure of speculating about other people's lives, we traveling men enjoyed the inns that we made our second homes. There was the Brandon Inn in Vermont with the wide, hospitable fireplace over which was the inscription:

> Whoe'er has travelled life's dull round,
> Whate'er his station may have been,
> May sigh to think he yet has found
> His warmest welcome in an inn.

I liked this so well that I decided when I built a house I would have a fireplace just like it, and I even wrote a verse for it. The verse I still have, but I never did get around to building the fireplace.

Then there were the Connecticut House in Waterbury, the Garde in New Haven, and the Hooker in Willimantic. In the morning when we knights of the grip started out we would say to one another, "Be in Waterbury tonight and we will have a game of pitch," and we would try to make our schedule fit.

One night as we were sitting at supper in the Connecticut House the talk turned on a story that was running in the New York *Journal* about the colony at West Athens, Maine, and old Abe whom the members used to yoke up with a steer for plowing. According to the story, the women drove him in a pung when they went to the store.

Someone said it was a lie. Someone else said, "This man is from Maine and he should know," so they demanded that I tell them whether or not old Abe was treated as though he were a horse.

I said there was a colony of queer people at West Athens, that Abe was weak in the head and strong in the arm, and that at times he undoubtedly was used as a beast of burden.

One man said, "What I want to know is whether or not they drive him to town."

"They used to, but they don't now," I answered. "The storekeeper made them stop. They used to drive him down and hitch him to a tree while they did their trading, but he gnawed all the bark off a big maple and killed it; so the villagers made them keep him at home."

Nobody could top that one for a few minutes, so we adjourned to our game.

Even the saddest hotels furnished us something to laugh about; and no matter how uncomfortable we were, we made our own entertainment. The hotel that topped all others in New England for general cussedness was the one at White River, which we couldn't avoid because it was a railroad junction. Nearly all the trains seemed to make White River at about midnight, so it was the custom of the innkeeper to speed the parting guest, change the sheets on the beds, and let the rooms to the men who came in on the same train that carried away the former occupants. At least that was the theory, but most of the time he didn't get around to changing the sheets.

The innkeeper's utter indifference to our comfort made him famous. One night I heard a furious guest charge out of the dining room and present a claim for damages.

"Look at what your table girl did to me. She has ruined my new suit. She has spilled cream all over it."

The proprietor didn't look up from his register.

"That's a lie," he grunted. "There hain't been no cream in this house for three years."

In White River Junction our entertainment was a bit rough and slapstick, but it did serve to relieve the dreariness of the place. One night at supper I sat next to a young kitchenware salesman who looked pretty lonely and down in the mouth. As soon as the waitress came over to slop a little water in our glasses she fixed him with a baleful glance and demanded, "I want my umbrella."

"Come up and get it," answered the young salesman.

"If you don't give it to me, I'm going to the proprietor, and you'll see what he will do."

"Go right ahead," urged the young man with a grin, trying to extract what fun he could from the situation.

The girl took our order and flounced out. I asked the boy what was all this about the umbrella, and he said that the girl had given him a glad eye, he had taken her to a show and supper, only to be told afterward that there was nothing doing. He wasn't the first man she had fooled, so he carried her umbrella up to his room and told her if she wanted it to come up and get it.

When the girl came back and began again about the umbrella, I got into the game.

"I am legal counsel for this poor, deluded young man," I said. "He has just confided to me the details of his transaction with you, and I have advised him that he has a good cause of action against you for cheating by false pretenses. He has left the matter in my hands, and I will be glad to defend any action you may bring against him."

But I couldn't fool that girl; she had met too many drummers. As she slammed the pie on the table, she hissed, "Go to hell, both of you."

It was at White River Junction that I tried to teach the proprietor's wife to make citron preserves. In Maine citron isn't the stuff you put in cake but a small melon good for nothing except to make a kind of preserves that has always been my first choice among the jars in the jam closet—also my second.

One rainy fall day when I was marooned in White River and had nothing else to do, I got a few of these little melons, which are as striped as a rattlesnake, as large as a cannonball, and as hard as Pharaoh's heart, and took them out to the pantry. From the proprietor's wife I borrowed a large, heavy meat knife and a stick of firewood and began to slice the melons, while the woman stood out of the way of the bombardment. She watched me with wary and skeptical interest, but found an ice pick with which I could punch out the seeds, all that were visible when I held the slices to the light.

When I had peeled and diced the slices, the woman filled a kettle with a few inches of boiling water and gave me a steamer to set over it. I tossed in the melon and let it steam until I could run a broomstraw through it; then I weighed the citron, added one lemon sliced thin and three-quarters of a pound of sugar for each five pounds of citron, and made a heavy syrup. When I began to skim off the seeds, the woman said cruelly, "I thought you got them all out with the pick," but I didn't say anything and hung over the kettle until my face was steaming and my arm had a crick in it. Every time I stirred, more seeds came up.

When I couldn't get another seed I put the preserve in a jar to cool and gave the woman a taste. A beatific smile spread over her face, but only for a minute.

"It's good," she admitted, "but only a fool would go to all that trouble. You'll never get a woman to make it for you." And she was right, I never did; whenever I wanted citron preserves I had to make them myself.

In White River Junction one might be driven to do anything, but usually there were two or three of us stranded together, so we found some way of entertaining ourselves even if we were reduced to exchanging stories about the ways we managed to get ahead of the home office. Personally, I never did pad my expense account unless I was driven to it; but however scrupulous I was, the treasurer always found some item of expense to complain about. Once I was goaded into telling him that if it was his idea that my job was to save money for the firm, the best way he could do it was to take me off the road. That kept him quiet for a while.

One traveler I met told how he had charged an item for taking a customer to a show, and the treasurer made a great howl about it. The next week when the drummer was given his money, the treasurer said, "I didn't see any item this week for entertainment." As the drummer put his money in his pocket, he answered, "No, you didn't see it, but it was there just the same."

Our favorite story at that time was about the new man that a company sent to Maine to make one trip for their old salesman, who was sick. When he came back to the office, the treasurer said the young fellow had forgotten to charge for a team to Vinalhaven and he should have included it, as the old man always did. The salesman was on the spot. He didn't like to point out that Vinalhaven is an island about ten miles offshore.

One of our chief sources of entertainment in Maine was figuring out the landlord's contrivances to get around prohibition. At that time Maine was so dry that it was illegal even to give liquor away, so a great many men were engaged in relieving the drought. In some counties the arms of the law merely insisted that liquor should be kept out of sight, but in Franklin County the sheriff was so zealous in his enforcement of the law that immense fortunes were being made in "Kentucky hardware."

One of the shrewdest schemes I ever saw worked by a bootlegger was operated at the Stoddard House in Farmington, a place that had a rather lurid history but was a favorite stopping place for traveling men, not only because they could wet their palates but also because the landlord was a pleasant fellow who set a good table and studied the wants of his guests.

This is the way he operated: When the depot hack drove up, the grips of all the drummers were piled in the lobby; when a man wanted his he picked it out, and it was taken to his room. One morning, when the grips were all dumped in front of the desk, one of the newcomers whispered a few words in the proprietor's ear. He went at once to the bags, selected one, and said, "I'll show you to your room." The two went upstairs together. In a few minutes the landlord and the guest came back down the stairs and placed the grip with the others. It wasn't hard to guess what the grip had contained.

If the sheriff ever happened to raid the place and the landlord were caught with this particular grip in his hand, he could say that it belonged to a drummer, and it would be exceedingly difficult to identify the drummer. The law could believe the tale or not. I never heard that the landlord was caught, and he operated for a long time.

Contrary to the usual opinion, not many drummers were given to the intemperate use of liquor; but we did like to see the sheriff work his head off trying to fathom how someone was hiding his stuff. Our favorite character was old Levi Coombs, the sheriff of Lisbon, who was on the trail of law-breakers by night and by day. As fast as the local rum runners evolved a new scheme of getting liquor in, Levi discovered their secrets and pounced on them.

Levi was also the proprietor of a small hardware store that made an excellent warehouse for confiscated goods, as it had no rear entrance or window. At night the front windows were covered with massive shutters and secured on the inside with one-inch bolts. There was only one key, and Levi never let it out of his pocket.

The sessions of the court were Levi's big moment, for it was a sure thing that the judge would order the liquor spilled. Nothing gave Levi such fiendish delight as the chance to smash kegs and jugs out in the street in plain sight of the thirsty. On one such occasion he presented his evidence, the court ordered the liquor spilled, and Levi prepared to carry out the mandate. In the presence of an unusual crowd of witnesses he swung his ax and smashed the head of the first keg. It was as empty as a bass drum. The crowd howled with delight at the sheriff's look of bafflement. Levi began to smell a large rat when he swung the ax again and the second keg was empty. More shouts of derision. The entire lot was as dry as a keg of nails.

Levi puzzled over his humiliation for a long time, until a friend gave him a clue. He had been betrayed by his own son, Bill, a twelve-year-old hellion who had borrowed his father's gimlet, collected a supply of bottles, and gone into the liquor business. He had peddled the whole supply at a very nice profit.

Old Levi was scandalized; he started home and met Bill coming out of the gate. The sheriff wrenched off one of the pickets from his fence, seized Bill, and began to administer some old-fashioned discipline. At the first whack Bill almost tore himself away and screamed "Stop! Stop!" but his cries only spurred Levi to greater effort. Finally Bill made him understand that there was a nail in that picket. Poor Bill was so lacerated that the most rabid temperance agitators were satisfied, but Levi's career was blighted; he gave up his attempts to preserve the aridity of Lisbon.

Whenever we traveling men spoke of Levi and his battle with the forces of evil we used to speculate about the future of Bill, whose superior talents seemed to be heading him straight for Big Business or the penitentiary. We used to invent episodes in his rise and fall; but how near we hit it I never knew. The last we heard of Bill was his adventure with Horace-by-God's horse, and he got out of that so easily that he seemed to be blessed by luck.

Horace had an old horse that was noted for his ability to sleep standing up. He would brace his feet and hang his head, then he was set for the day. One morning Horace stopped on his way to town to make a trade with one of his neighbors. As usual, his horse went to sleep at the side of the road. That was the morning Bill chose to take out his father's fast little strip-faced bay, with which the latter used to chase the enemy. He had not asked Levi's permission. As he was making a 2.30 gait down the Lewiston road, he swung around the corner and collided with Horace-by-God's horse. The shaft of his buggy, which had been worn down to a point, struck the old sleeping horse in the breast and nearly pierced him through. Horace came out, viewed the heap of wreckage, and demanded who was going to pay for his horse. As Levi showed no inclination to do it, claiming that Bill had taken the horse without his authority, Horace sued. But the court upheld Levi's views. We always felt a bit sorry for Horace.

FISHERMAN'S FAVORITE

I ALWAYS liked to go to Fort Kent in late April when the snow had melted and the timber came down. Then it looked very different from the scene of our winter revels.

Upstream the woodsmen, who had been cutting and yarding up the timber since September, had finished hauling the logs to the shore. I had stopped at their winter camps and eaten their beanhole beans baked in the earth, the best beans ever turned out by the hand of man. I had watched them making their wagon-sled roads to the landing, scattering marsh hay on the ramdowns to check the movement of the loads when the descent was too steep, or sometimes letting the loads down with a snub warp attached to the sleds by a turn or two taken around a stump and a man told off to hold the turn and prevent the team from being sluiced.

Of a morning after the water sled had poured a stream of water onto the track late the night before, I had seen them haul down enormous loads and had stood around shivering while they started the load in the yards by bumping the runners of the sled with a log swung from an arm. Then the horses sat down on their haunches and away they went down to the river.

Once I happened to be in a camp when the ice broke up and the whole landing started with a roar. I followed down-river, where picked men of the crew stood in melting ice water up to their waists waiting to dislodge jammed logs at strategic spots, working for hours at a time until the rear of the drive came along and they could snatch a chance to get some beans and coffee and doughnuts. Then they hung their wet mittens to dry over the blazing fire near the cookwagon and lay down in their wet clothes on piles of boughs covered with woods quilts and slept until morning. It was an article of faith with lumbermen to dry their clothes on them if they didn't want to catch cold. I have tried it, and it works; so I offer it for the consideration of all boys whose mothers say, "Come right in the house and get those wet clothes off, or you will catch your death of cold."

And, by the way, don't believe it when you read about the calk boots of the lumbermen. The driver wears low-cut, serviceable shoes with soles driven full of sharp calks to give him a firm grip on the logs; but high boots—foolish! Who wants to carry around all day a high boot full of water!

There was an excitement about a timber drive that made it for me the most fascinating show on earth, and the drive that I saw the spring of the big log jam at the Fort Kent bridge was one of the greatest of them all. The moment I got in and heard about it I walked down to the best vantage point, the suspension bridge that an enterprising saloonkeeper in Clair, the village across the river, had built across the stream. The exit was in his barroom. He collected a tidy sum from the teetotalers but charged no toll to the patrons of his bar.

The logs were piled up from the bottom of the river to a height of forty feet above the surface, and the rick extended upriver for a thousand yards. The river had dropped a little from freshet pitch, and it looked like an impossible job to start the jam. By the time I got there, the river drivers had dug out a space that stretched nearly a hundred yards from the bridge. As the head of the jam was lodged on one of the piers, they were afraid to use dynamite for fear they would destroy the bridge, so they were trying to dig the logs out, letting them drift downstream.

When they found a key log, several of them clamped on it with their peaveys and lifted. As it gave, part of the jam would fall apart and the men would clamber upward to safety if they could. A man in a boat held onto the pier with a rope, ready to drop it in an instant to rescue a driver who might be swept into the water, but I didn't see a single one lose his footing. Again and again the drivers climbed up the crumbling front of that precipice of moving logs, until it seemed that nothing could keep them from being drawn under the avalanche, and always by some superhuman feat they managed to save themselves.

An old Frenchman who was standing beside me leaned over the rail to watch a boat that popped into view for a moment and then was swept under the bridge and out of sight.

"Me, I know dese feller," he said. "She live way down river by Van Buren. She been all winter by Five Island. I bet you a dollar dere's ten t'ousand lice in dat boat." I didn't take him up on it, as I was afraid he was right.

After finishing in Fort Kent I went on down to New Sweden, where a Norwegian ran a little inn that had good beds and an excellent cook. Other traveling men knew about it, so I wasn't surprised to find there another implement man and a hardware salesman from Bangor. We planned, as we usually did when we were in Aroostook or the Rangeleys, to get in a fishing trip. The ice was barely out of the lakes, and it was cold; but we thought we were tough enough to take it, so we got a sixteen-year-old French boy for a guide and invited the landlord to come along.

We left our team at Guerette, a village on one of the Eagle

Lakes, and took a boat for the trip up the river that connects
with the lake at the head of the chain. It was running banks
full, so we had a good workout at the oars. When we stopped
to rest at the foot of a gigantic hemlock, I noticed a pile of
fishbones as clean as though they had been boiled, and I
couldn't account for them. The French boy pointed to a
fish hawk perching on a limb above us and said the bones
were the remains of a young salmon he had eaten for dinner.

It was dark by the time we reached Long Lake and landed
on a point where, years earlier, lumbermen had built a group
of cabins. We had hoped to find them habitable, but they
were in ruins; so we made a lean-to against the best one, put
a piece of canvas over it, and tore down the worst of the
camp for firewood. In a few minutes we had a fire going and
coffee boiling.

The French boy, abetted by the Norwegian, filled us up
with stories that made goose-pimples come out on the other
two salesmen, who were new to the North Woods—tales
about porcupines that lie in wait for you by the trails and
shoot you full of quills, and the side-hill ranger that had
two long legs on one side and two short ones on the other
to get around quickly on hillsides. When a ranger charges
you, your only salvation is to turn and run the other way,
because when he reverses he can't stand up. They dwelt on
the swamp swogon, whose scream is certain death to all who
hear him. And the wolverine that the Chippewas called
Ipewang, "the greedy," because in the winter when all other
animals are denned up he even attacks the porcupine, quills
and all. The quills stick in his mouth and stomach, and in a
few days he dies.

"Dis old Indian debbil, him a killer," the French boy told
us. "Him no sense like de bear an' de wolf. Dey watch till
dey see a porcupine rolled up asleep in de snow, den dey

roll him over an' rip him down the belly wit' one stroke. After him dead, dey skin him so neat as a trapper do it, an' eat him. Dey don't get stuck up by de quills."

All this talk about side-hill rangers and swogons and Ipewangs wasn't calculated to make us sleep too soundly, so one of the boys took an ax to bed with him, and the other an immense iron bar with a bolt on it that would crush the skull of an elephant. In the middle of the night I heard a great scuffling and tearing in the fish barrels on the other side of the camp wall, and thought probably it was a hedge-hog, which is very fond of salt; so I sat up, lit a match, and shouted to frighten the marauder away. As there was a great hole in the wall, the animal was within about six feet of me with nothing between us. Instead of retreating, it set up the most bloodcurdling screams I have ever heard. The hardware man grabbed his ax, and the other felt for his bar. Their eyes were as big as cannonballs, and white in the flicker of the match.

The creature began to move off, and its screams died in the woods. The boy called out, "Let her go. She's an old fisher with a mess of young 'uns, and she'd try to eat you alive if you went after her." He threw a log of half-rotted spruce on the fire, and we all rolled over, hoping to go to sleep.

At about half past three I was awakened by the sound of a man driving a stake. For a moment I wondered what could be going on, then I remembered the "stake driver," the blue heron that stands in the sedge and rushes, uttering this cry as he hunts for frogs. It was a lonesome sound. As I lay there looking out over the black lake, believing myself miles from human habitation, I heard a whistle tooting, a thin whe-e-e. This was really a whistle; no animal I had ever heard of made such a sound. The dawn was just beginning to break. In a few minutes a group of misty figures, men and women, came down out of the woods to the water's edge, got into a boat, pulled out into the lake, and boarded a little steamer that puffed out of the mist. Behind it were trailing a number of little boats like the one that had carried these phantoms.

As the steamer puffed back into the gray mist and whistled its eery whe-e-e for another landing, I wakened the guide and asked what was going on. These woods around the lake were full of French Canadians, he told me, who lived in this wilderness without a road or any contact with civilization except the lake. In the winter they traveled on the ice, in the summer by boat, but there was a period before the ice was strong enough to bear in the fall and before it went out in the spring when they were completely isolated. This morning they were going to church thirteen miles down the lake. They owned the steamer in common, probably forty or fifty of them, and never missed a Sunday when the lake was open or the ice would bear.

The Norwegian, who heard us talking, added that the church was the whole life of the people. In the little village of Guerette, where we had left the buggy, the priest had established the first cooperative society in these parts, and it was doing wonders to lift the standard of living of his parishioners.

Soon we were all awake, and by daylight were on the lake fishing; but we had no luck, for a strong wind came up and nearly swamped us as we moved into the river.

On this trip I wound up by doing the cooking, as I usually did, and made for supper my favorite lobscouse and steak. Maybe you don't know lobscouse. It is a fisherman's dish with many aliases. I fry out a big supply of salt pork or bacon in a deep kettle, and while the pork is frying I drop into the hot fat about four good-sized onions, peeled and sliced. While they are frying I peel and slice the same number of good-sized potatoes, add pepper and salt and a cup of water, and cover the kettle as tightly as possible to steam-cook the potatoes. I leave the bacon scraps in the kettle, and stir the whole a few times to see that the potatoes and onions are well mixed. When the potatoes are cooked through I shout once, and then stand aside to avoid the rush—for the pork fat and the water blend into a gravy that can't be beat.

Of course the proper thing to serve with this is steak broiled on a rock stove over a bed of dead alders that have washed down and lodged in the bushes and have dried out until they are just right. The steak should be about four inches from the fire, and as soon as it is seared on one side it should be seared on the other, then turned for about seven minutes. With a pound of steak apiece for supper and a pint of lobscouse, no fisherman will starve before morning.

On another fishing trip to Fall Brook Lake I came upon one of the most interesting sights that I had found in the North Woods. We were in an automobile, and as we approached the ferry that was to take us across the Allegash River we frightened a horse that tore down the road in front of us and plunged into the river. A cream-separator salesman who was along stood up and began to shout, "Somebody pull him out, he'll drown," but the guide quieted him. These were river horses, he said, and nobody could drown them, for they spent their lives in the water pulling flatboats loaded with supplies up over the rapids to the lumber camps.

As we stood on the bank waiting for the ferry we saw one of these boats start out with a ten-ton load that it looked impossible for a team to move, but the horses pulled it upstream belly deep in the water and managed to keep their footing on the slippery rocks while the boat moved stolidly behind. The guide said they sometimes towed their loads as far as a hundred miles upstream; then they were put aboard the flatboat and slid home.

THE PAYOFF

*B*EFORE I had been on the new job very long the manager called me in to tell me some great news. The company had sold two of our newest patents for handsome sums to rival companies; the Low Down spreader, which had the beater hung on the main axle, had gone to the John Deere Company, and the Easy Loader, which had a side that dropped down and enabled it to load easier, had gone to the Johnston Harvester Company.

And was the company pleased! I was pleased but not excited, because I was sure we had kept the best one. To my mind the last two were inventors' dreams that had features which might offset their advantages. I was too much of a Yankee to want to improve something that worked as well as the old spreader did.

Somehow, these contraptions that the chief of our experimental department dreamed up always made me think of the invention of the man I met at Durham. The fellow owned a threshing machine and used to go out threshing grain for all and sundry. One year he extended his route so far that winter overtook him and he was forced to send for sleds to haul his machine home. This waste of time and money struck him as needless, so he began to work on an idea for a set of sleds that could be hung under his threshing machine. When they were needed, they were to be released by a lever and dropped down to take the burden instead of the wheels.

After working all summer, the man had his sleds finished and ready for a tryout. He pulled the lever and held his breath to watch the sleds come down, but nothing happened. Then he crawled under his contraption with a hammer and hit it a gosh-awful wallop. It came to life with a great thud, dropped about a ton of sleds on him, and nailed him to the barn floor as firmly as though he had been in a giant vise. His roars for help brought the neighbors.

"Get an ax," someone shouted.

"Don't none of you damn fools touch nothin'!" the inventor yelled. "If you do, I'll have the law on ye. You send and get Black John Coombs. He knows about machinery, and he'll get me out and not bust nothin'." So the man stayed there until Black John rescued him, but his invention met an untimely end, for his wife put the kibosh on it.

I won't go into the kinks in the patents that the company sold, but I didn't grieve overmuch to see them go. However, when I went back on the road I was greeted everywhere with the news that we were going out of business and had sold our best spreaders. My answer was the only logical one I could think of, "Did you ever know a farmer to sell his best cow?" This was reported promptly to the company, and did not increase my popularity in the office.

Not long after this I was sent to Aroostook County to try to stir up some business. There I saw that I would need a leader to get the carload trade; so I went into the inventing business myself and dreamed up a two-row horse hoe that would work two furrows at once. When our experimental department had built it, the president told me to sell it on six months' time, because a man might pay cash when he saw a new machine at work; but if he wouldn't pay for it six months later, the time to find out was right away, before the company had spent a lot of money making it.

The first man to whom I sold not only paid for it but ordered six more for his neighbors, so I was off for a big season's business. But just as my plans were working out, I had a letter from the company instructing me to leave Aroostook and go into Washington County, where there was nothing but blueberry barrens and sardine factories. I wanted to continue in Aroostook, but the company insisted that I had already sent in more business than they ever had received out of this county, and they were afraid the district might have a poor crop year. Definitely, they didn't want any more business from Aroostook.

When I saw that words were of no avail, I left for the new territory. No one who hasn't seen it can imagine the bleakness of Washington County in the dead of winter, when the men are in the woods lumbering and it is impossible to find anyone who wants to buy anything.

After wandering around a while, unable to find the remotest resemblance to business, I grew more and more dissatisfied with the whole thing. On Saturday night I ran into Machias, and at supper met a young man who told me about a splendid opening for a man who would like to buy out a general store in the town of Harmony. The more I inquired, the better it looked, so on Monday morning I set out for Harmony. When I came away I had a contract in my pocket.

I wrote the company that I had bought out a country store and that they might hold me to my contract, but I did not think they would want to, as I had lost interest and felt that I couldn't do them any good on the road. They did not make too much difficulty, and sometime the last of March I finished my labors.

As it turned out, it was just as well that I left the company, for not five years later the firm went on the rocks. Old Mr. Curtis was dead, and the new management did not have his keen mind and sound business sense. During the First World War the company united with several others, and they all went down together.

I am glad I quit the road. If I had remained I might have been successful as a traveling man, but no one ever gets very far whose every action is dictated by someone in the office. I had to learn to trust my own judgment; not because it was the best but because it was the only judgment I could find that was devoted entirely to my interests. I had learned, as one soon does, that when somebody says, "If I were in your place I would . . . ," very likely he is trying to get you to do something down his alley. If a man has ordinary judgment and learns to trust it, he will get along.

Now as I am nearing the end, I often think of the tyrant who, when he was on his deathbed, was told to forgive his enemies. He said he hadn't any, as he had killed them all. The Lord has killed mine by old age. I haven't a single enemy that I know of—so I want to wish everyone long life, good health, and a clear conscience. What more is there to ask for?